Sing It, Dance It, Play It, Learn It!

Songs for the Elementary Music Classroom

*A Collection of Songs That Teach Life Lessons
Through Music and Other Activities*

Sing It, Dance It, Play It, Learn It! Piano Accompaniments for Vol. 1
by Lea L. Landolfi and Dr. Neil M. Boumpani

Sevenhorns Publishing
A Division of SevenHorns, LLC
276 5th Avenue, Suite 704
New York, NY 10001
www.sevenhornspublishing.com

Copyright 2019 by Lea Landolfi and Neil Boumpani.

All rights reserved. Published in the United States by Sevenhorns Publishing, a division of SevenHorns, LLC.

The Sevenhorns name and logo are trademarks of SevenHorns, LLC.

This publication may be reproduced for classroom use only, and may not be distributed, or transmitted in any format, or by any means, or stored in a database or retrieval system for any other purpose without the prior written permission of the publisher.

Credits:
Author: Lea L. Landolfi
Editor: Brielle E. Bogdzio
Illustration Artist: Lea L. Landolfi
Book Cover Design: Lea L. Landolfi and Branded Human
Music Editor: Dr. Neil Boumpani

Manufactured in the United States of America

Library of Congress Control Number: 2018952227

ISBN: 978-0-9600817-6-9 (pbk.)

Visit www.LandBMusic.com

Sing It, Dance It, Play It, Learn It!

S.D.P.L. Series, Piano Accompaniments for Vol. 1

Table of Contents...

Table of Contents..iii
Notes on Accompaniments.....................vi

Song   **Page**

A Reggae Day……………………………………………………………………..…1

A Time for Everything…………………………………………………………….4

Be A Good Friend…………………………………………………………….…..8

Be Nice Rap…………………………………………………………………………11

Dance-a-mania………………………………………………………………….…15

Doin' My Best……………………………………………………………………..19

Doodles……………………………………………………………………………….22

Eat Right……………………………………………………………………………..25

Go To Bed……………………………………………………………………………27

How Are You?..30

Jump High, Jump Low…………………………………………………………33

Let's Play……………………………………………………………………………..37

Look Right, Look Left………………………………………………………….42

Move, Move, Move………………………………………………………………44

My Family……………………………………………………………………………49

Number Fun………………………………………………………………………..53

Paint Brush Blues ………………………………………………………………..55

Personality……………………………………………………………………………60

Please and Thank You………………………………………………………….66

Table of Contents...

Song   **Page**

Rainbow……………………………………………………………………………………………..69

Rules, Rules, Rules………………………………………………………………………………...75

Smile…………………………………………………………………………………………………78

Steady beat………………………………………………………………………………………….81

Tell the Truth………………………………………………………………………………………..84

The Learning Cha Cha……………………………………………………………………………..87

The Question………………………………………………………………………………………..92

Train Ride……………………………………………………………………………………………95

When I Grow Up…………………………………………………………………………………….97

Notes on the Piano Accompaniments

In order to create playable piano accompaniments we considered how we could best serve the teachers and students.
With this in mind, we set the following goals:

1. **To make the parts as playable as possible so that they can be played by most certified music educators.**

2. **Whenever possible, to include the melody in the accompaniment.** We achieved this with most, but not all, of the accompaniments.

3. **Whenever possible, to include important aspects of the recorded tracks.** Introductions, endings, background riffs, melodic links, etc., have been added wherever possible.

4. **To make sure that the "feel" of the music is firmly established.**

5. **To include chord symbols for those who wish to modify the written part or create or create their own accompaniments.**

We believe that, for the most part, we were able to reach these goals with all of our accompaniments. One notable exception is the rap tune *Be Nice*. We wrote the part thinking that the only instrument available to accompany this song would be a piano. Without percussion instruments, the bass part was modified to meet the rhythmic and stylistic aspects of the music.

We invite teachers to freely change any accompaniments to serve your individual needs. Please feel free to share suggestions at www.LandBMusic.com, and check out teaching videos on our YouTube channel.

A Reggae Day

Words and Music by
Lea L. Landolfi

COPYRIGHT © 2016 L. Landolfi and Boumpani Music Co., ASCAP

A Reggae Day

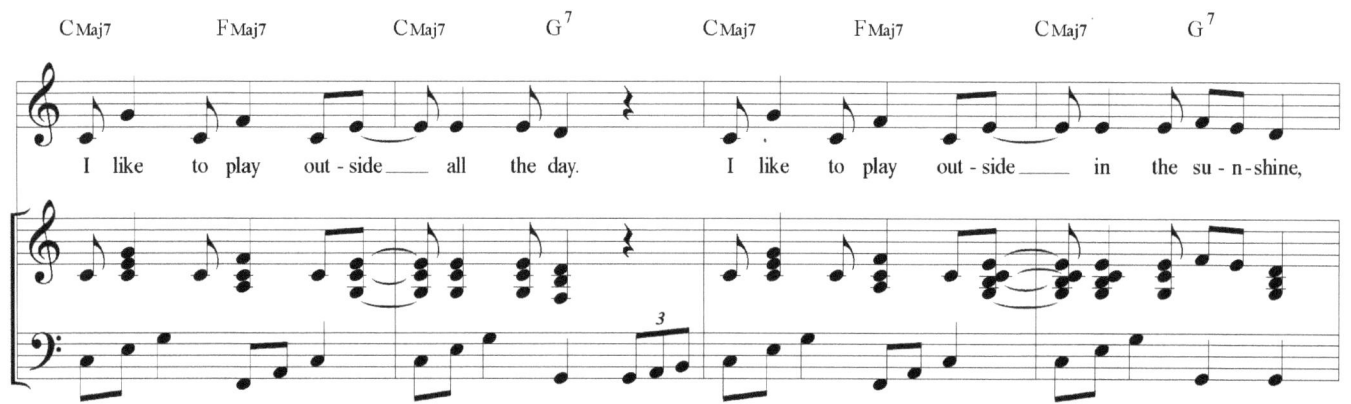

A Reggae Day

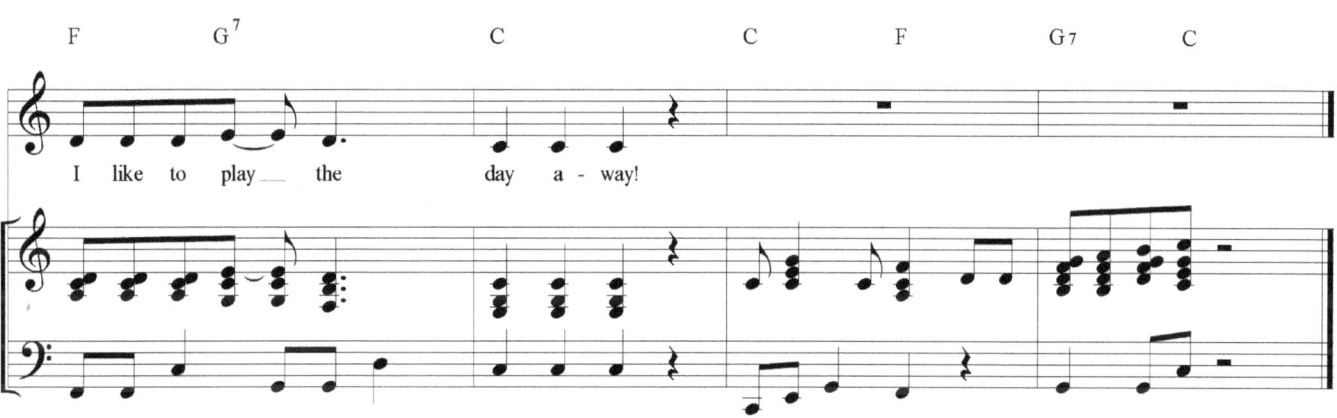

A Time For Everything

Words and Music by
Neil M. Boumpani
Lea L. Landolfi

COPYRIGHT © 2016 L. Landolfi and Boumpani Music Co. ASCAP

3 o-clock 4 o-clock 5 o-clock 6 o-clock 7 o-clock 8 o-clock 9 o-clock 10 o-clock
(one person)
D
E♭ cm
11 o-clock 12 o-clock coo-coo coo-coo coo-coo There's a time to learn there's a
fm7 B♭ B♭7 E♭ B♭ E♭ E♭ E♭7 E♭7+
time to play. There's a time for ev-'ry-thing to-day. If you read the clock then

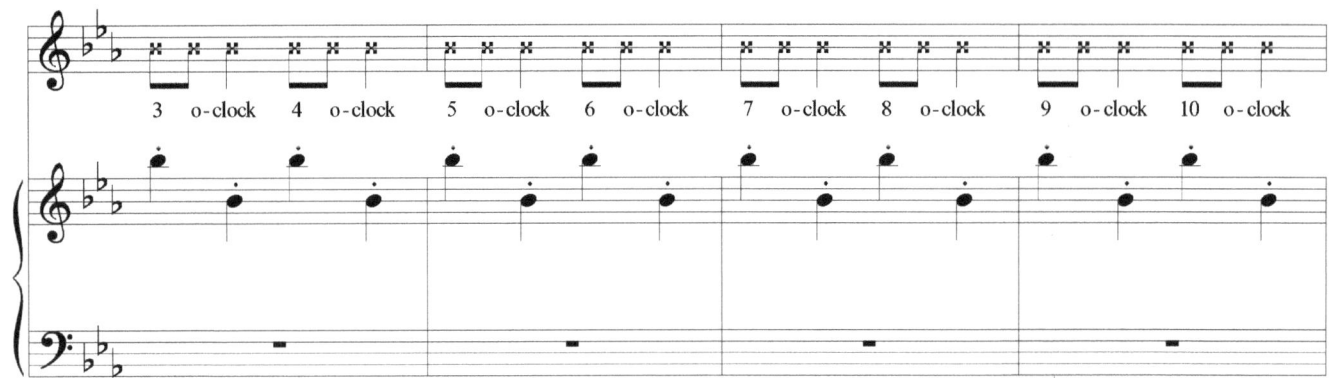

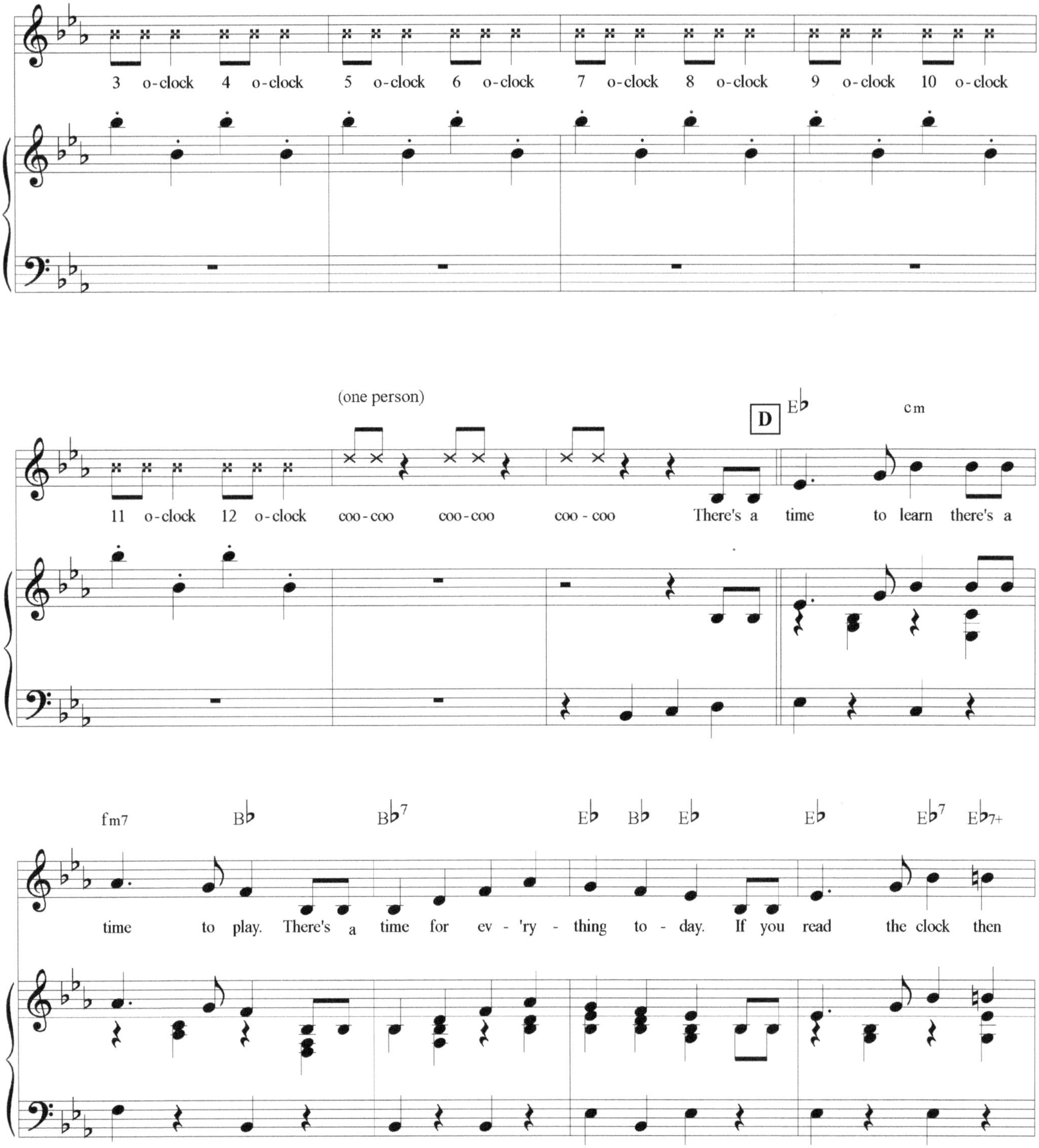

A Time For Everything

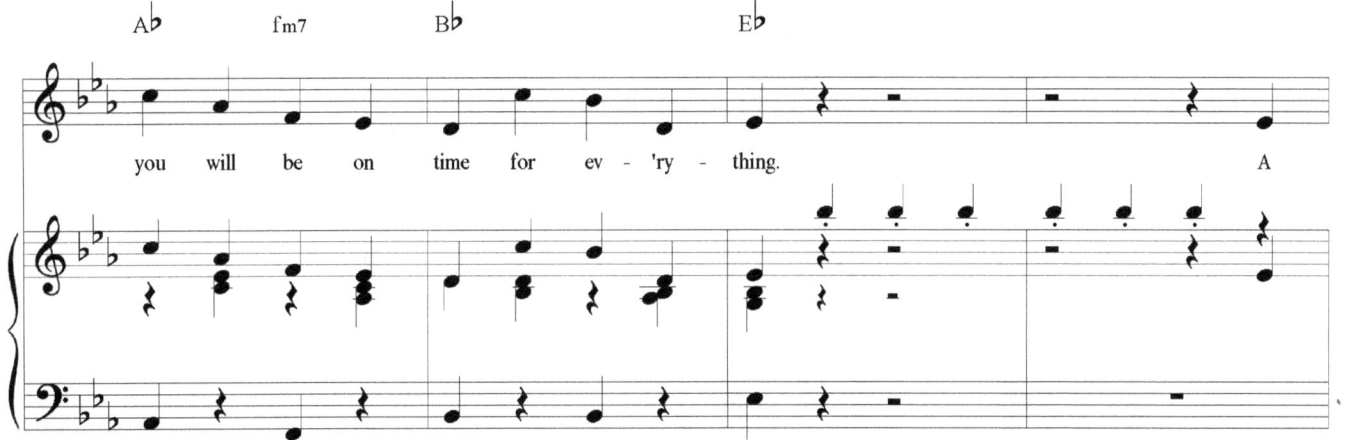

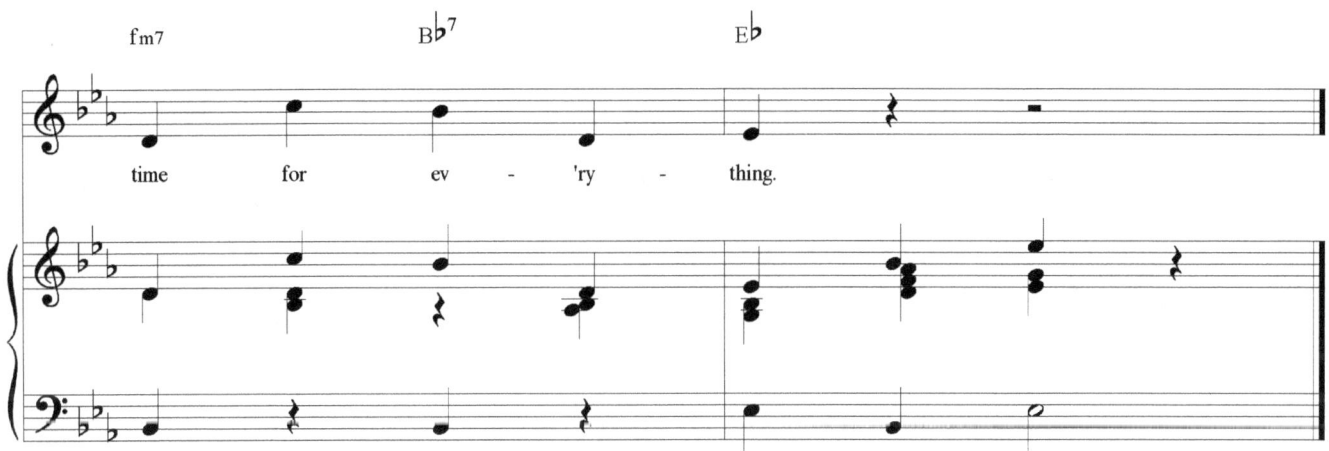

Be a Good Friend

Be a Good Friend

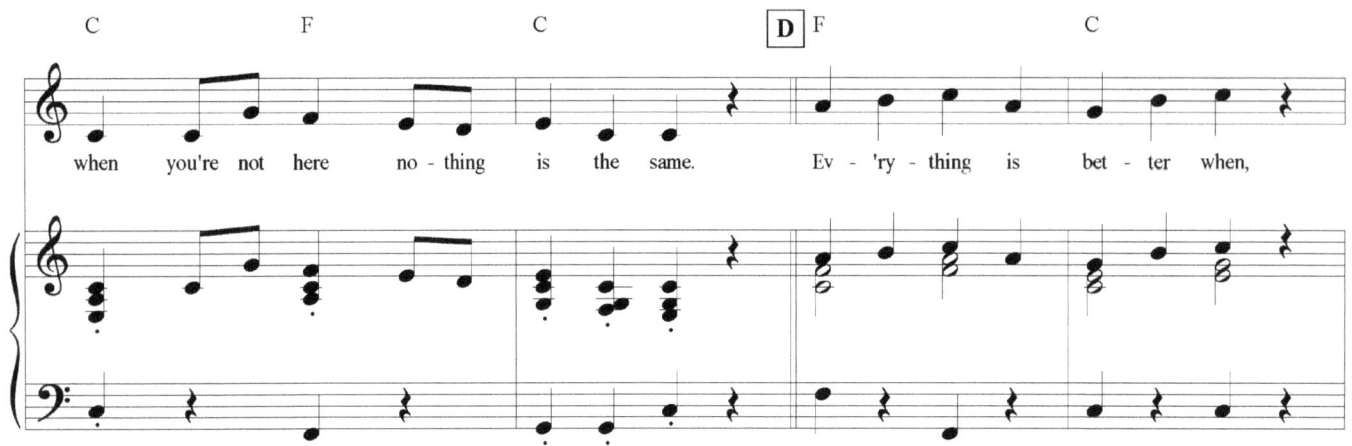
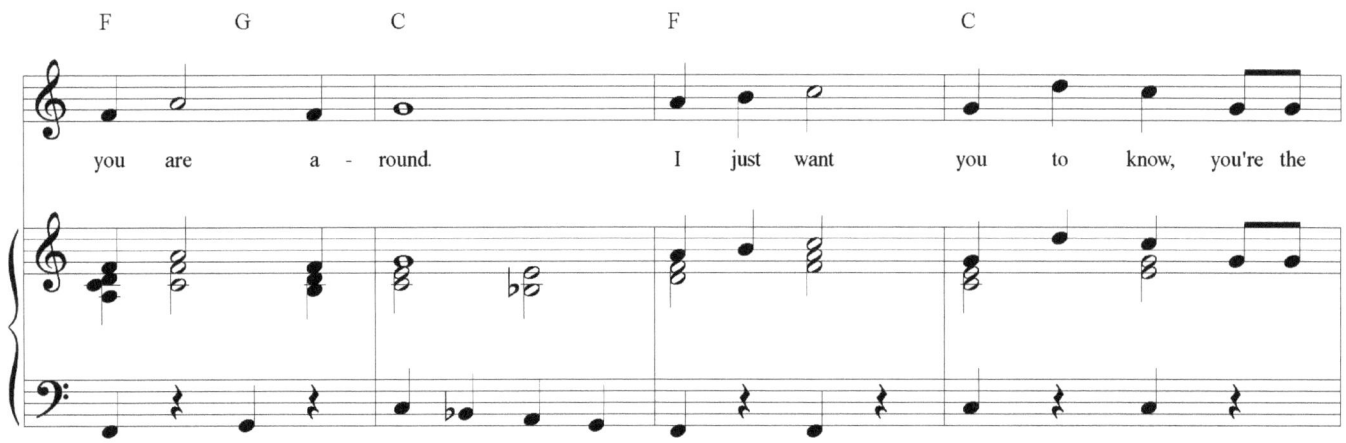

Be Nice

Words and Music by
Lea L. Landolfi

COPYRIGHT © 2016 L. Landolfi and Boumpani Music Co. ASCAP

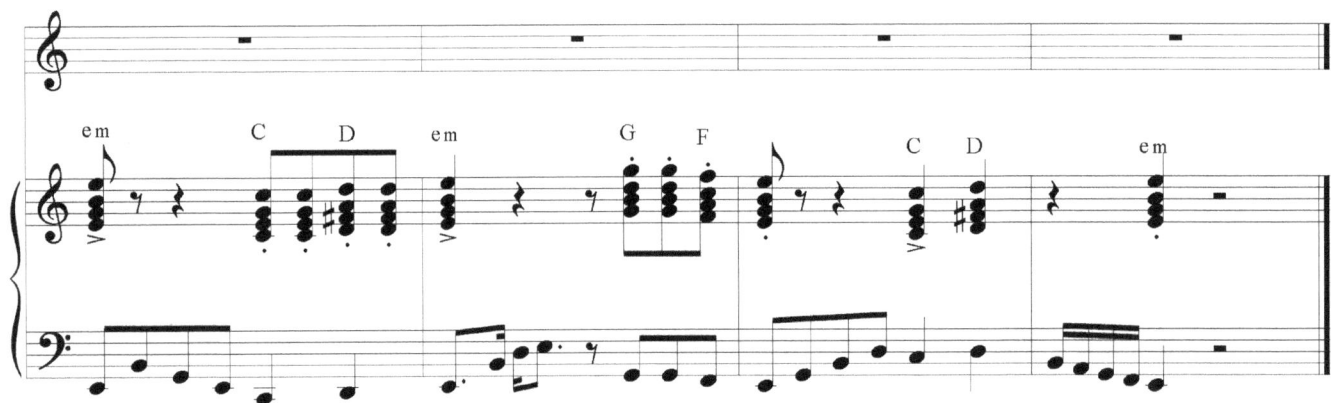

Dance-a-mania

Dance-a-mania

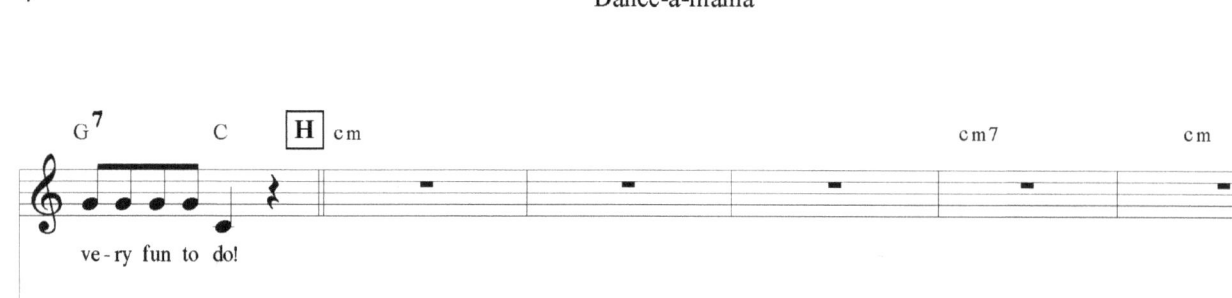

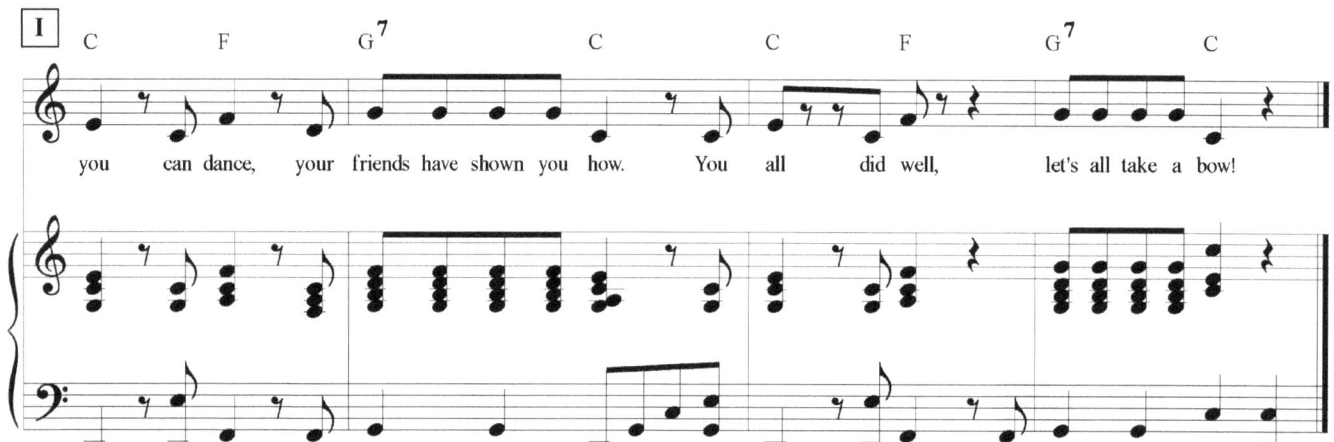

Doin' My Best

Words and Music by Lea L. Landolfi

COPYRIGHT © 2016 L. Landolfi and Boumpani Music Co. ASCAP

Doodles

Words and Music by
Lea L. Landolfi

COPYRIGHT © 2016 L. Landolfi and Boumpani Music Co. ASCAP

Doodles

Eat Right

Words and Music by
Lea L. Landolfi

COPYRIGHT © 2016 L. Landolfi and Boumpani Music Co. ASCAP

Go To Bed

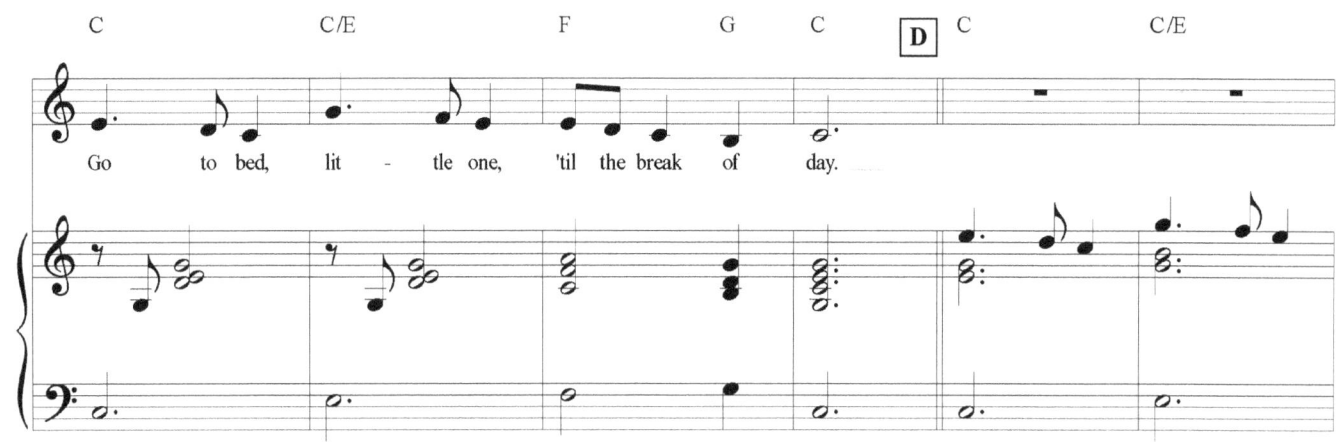

How Are You?

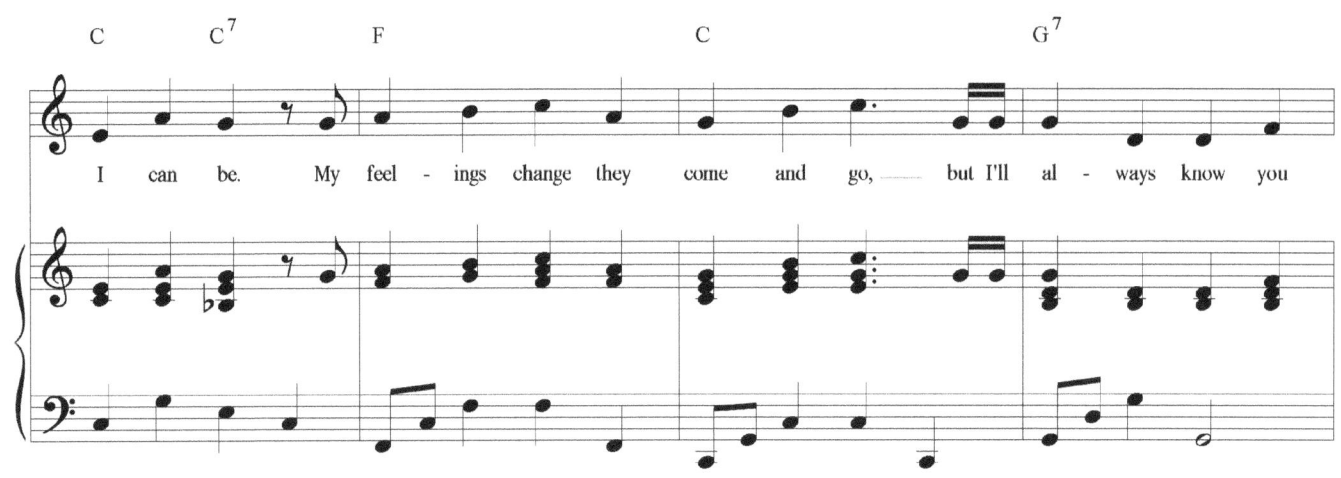

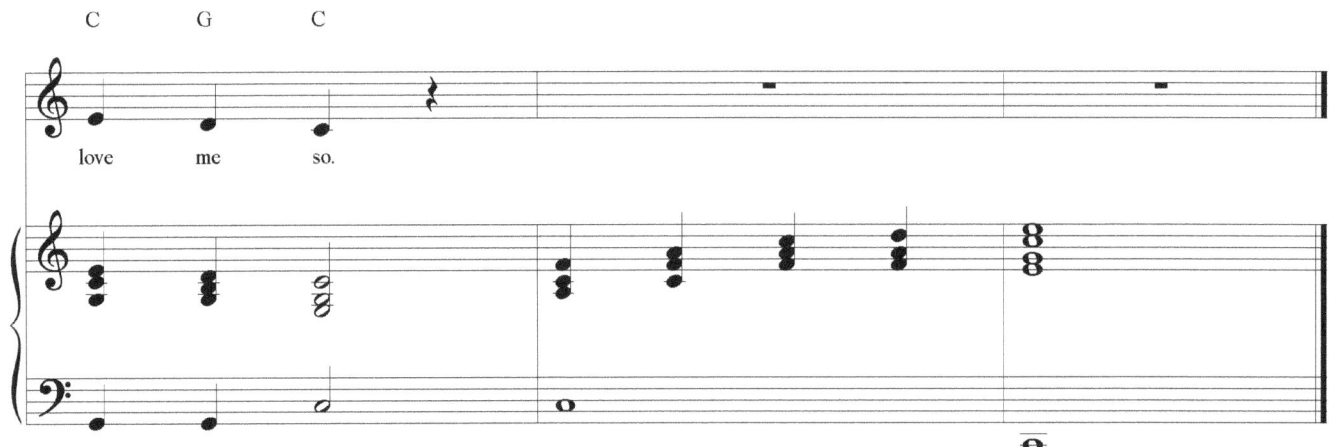

Jump High, Jump Low

Jump High, Jump Low

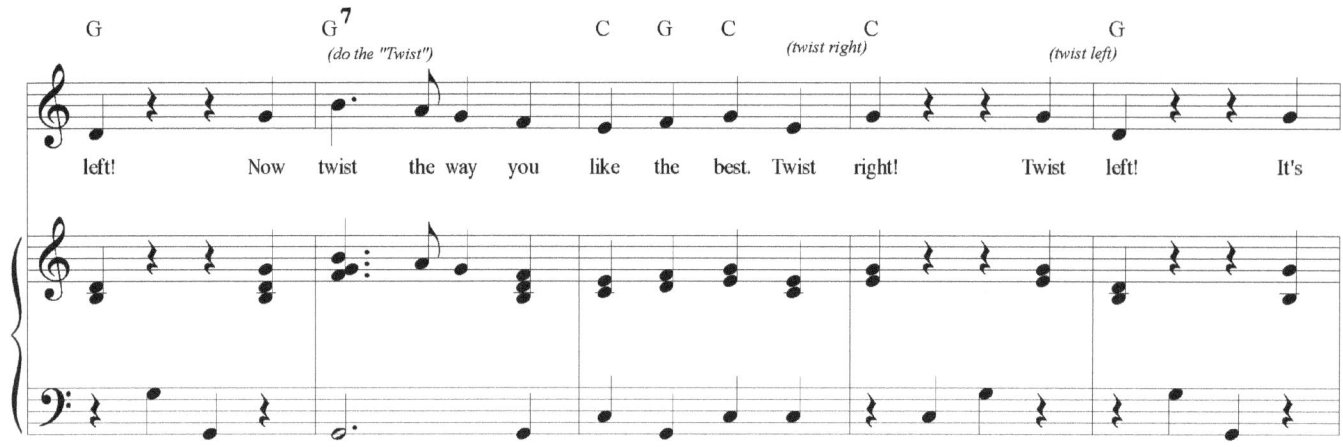
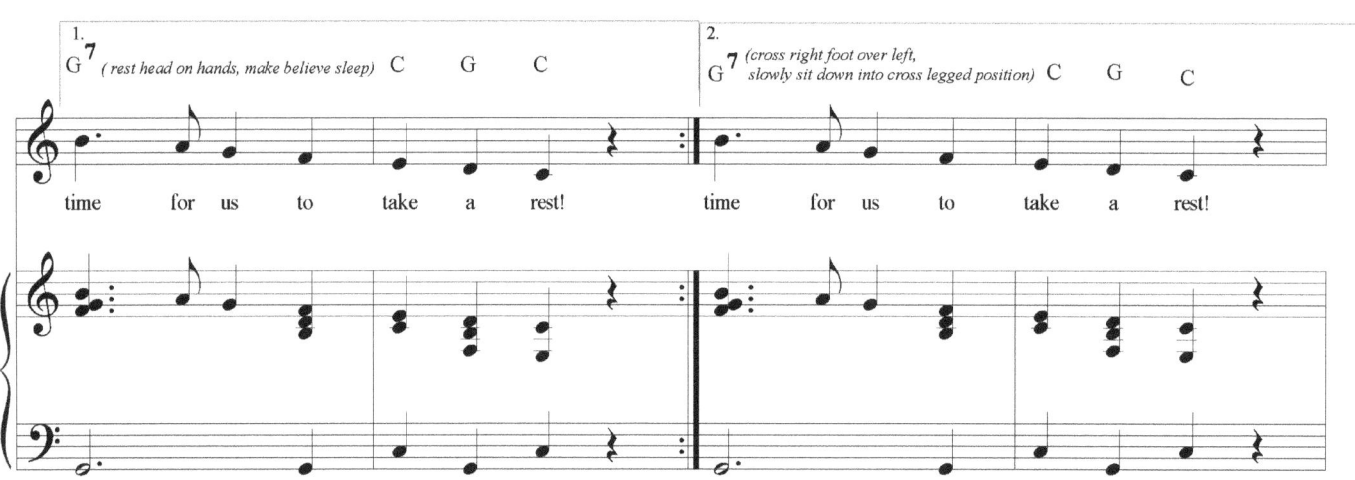

Let's Play

be such fun, but noth-in' beats a real home-run! Oh, it's a great day in the neigh-bor-hood. It's a

great day to play. Oh, it's a great day in the neigh-bor-hood. Stop wast-in' your life a-

way. Get off that couch go out and play. Do it now while it's still day. There's

Let's Play

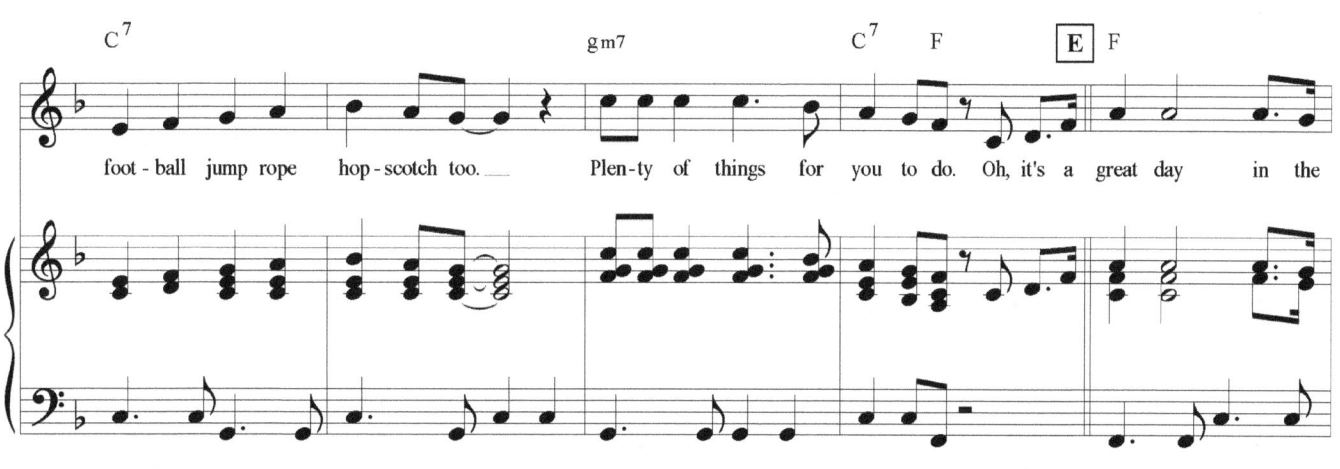

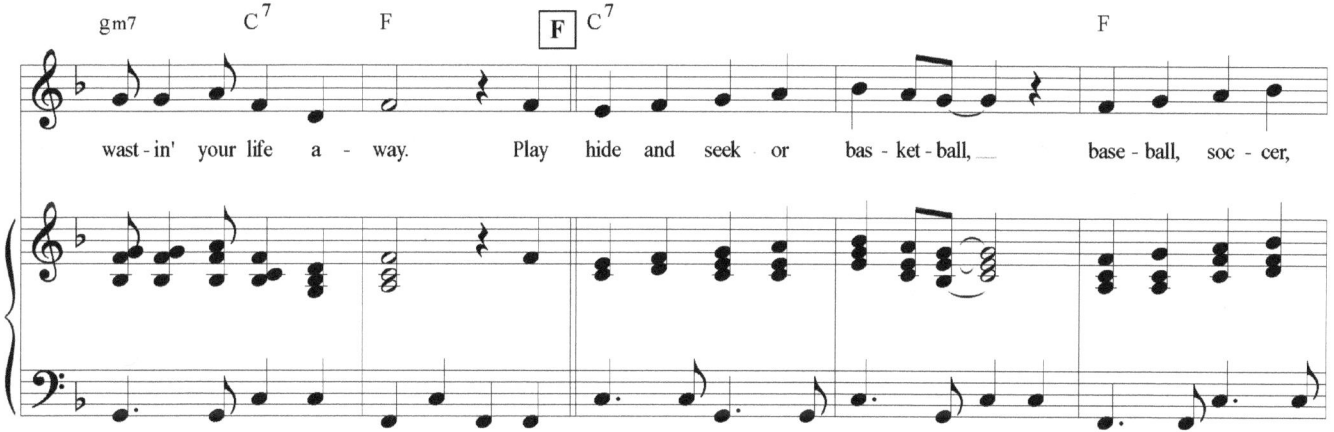

Let's Play

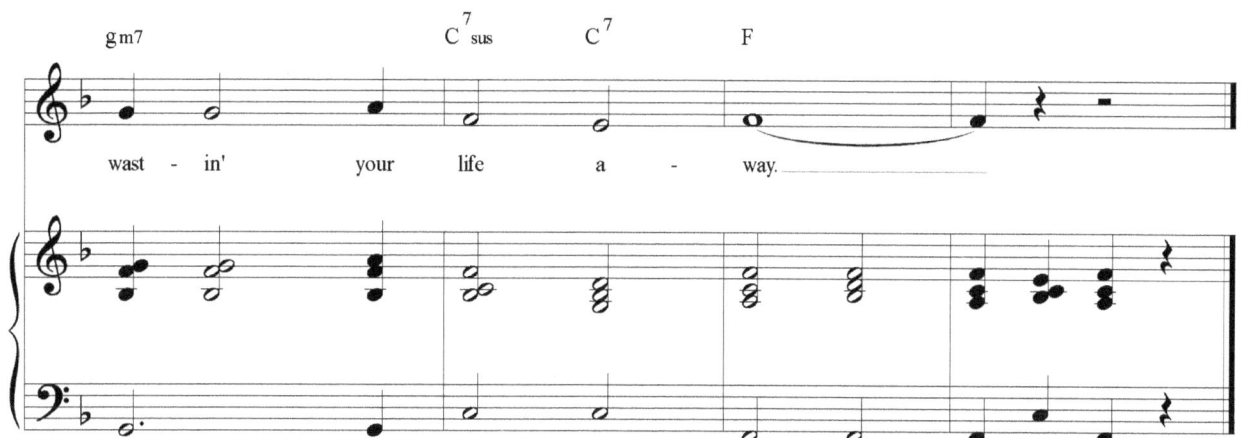

Look Right, Look Left

Words and Music by
Lea L. Landolfi

COPYRIGHT © 2016 L. Landolfi and Boumpani Music Co. ASCAP

Move Move Move

Words and Music by
Lea L. Landolfi

Move Move Move

Move Move Move

My Family

Words and Music by
Lea L. Landolfi

My Family

Number Fun

Words and Music by Lea L. Landolfi

COPYRIGHT © 2016 L. Landolfi and Boumpani Music Co. ASCAP

Number Fun

G7 C C dm C G7 C F C G7 C
now it's time to shut the door. Five and six and sev - en eight, hur - ry up now don't be late. One, two, tie your shoe.
F C G7 C F C G7 C G7 C
Three, four, shut the door. Five and six, sev - en, ei - ght, nine ten!
C dm C/E C G7 C

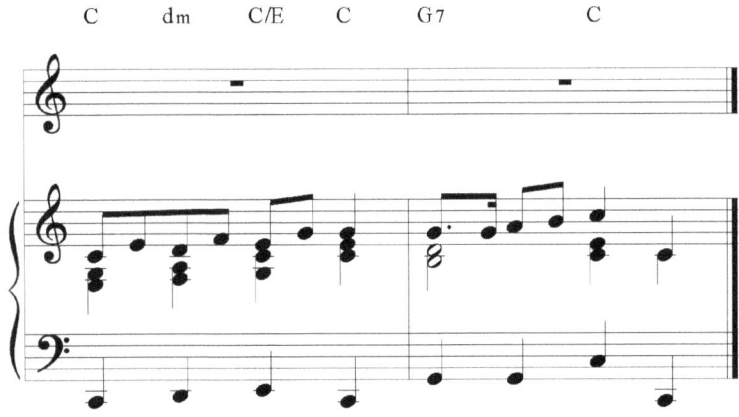

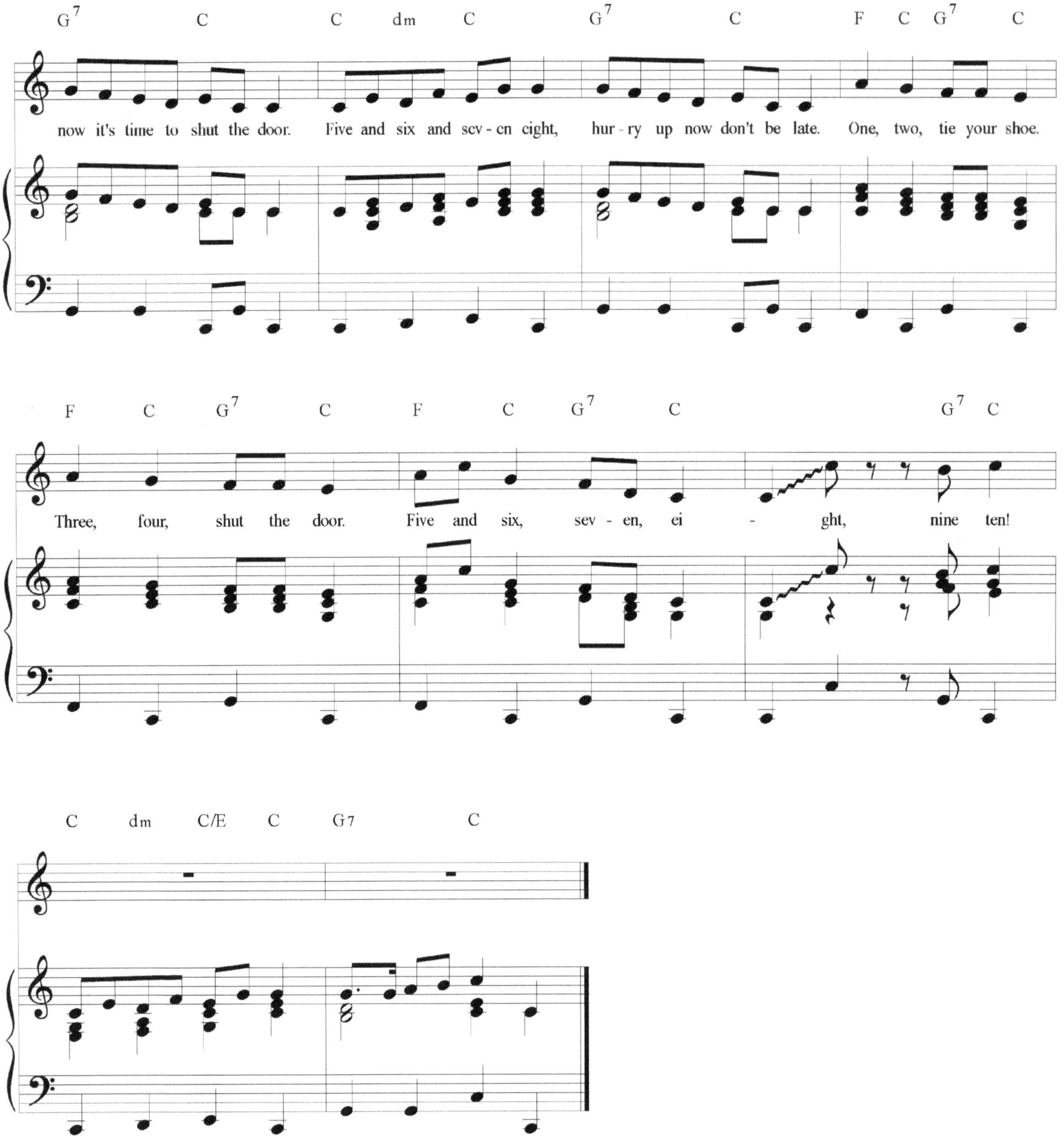

Paint Brush Blues

Words and Music by
Lea L. Landolfi

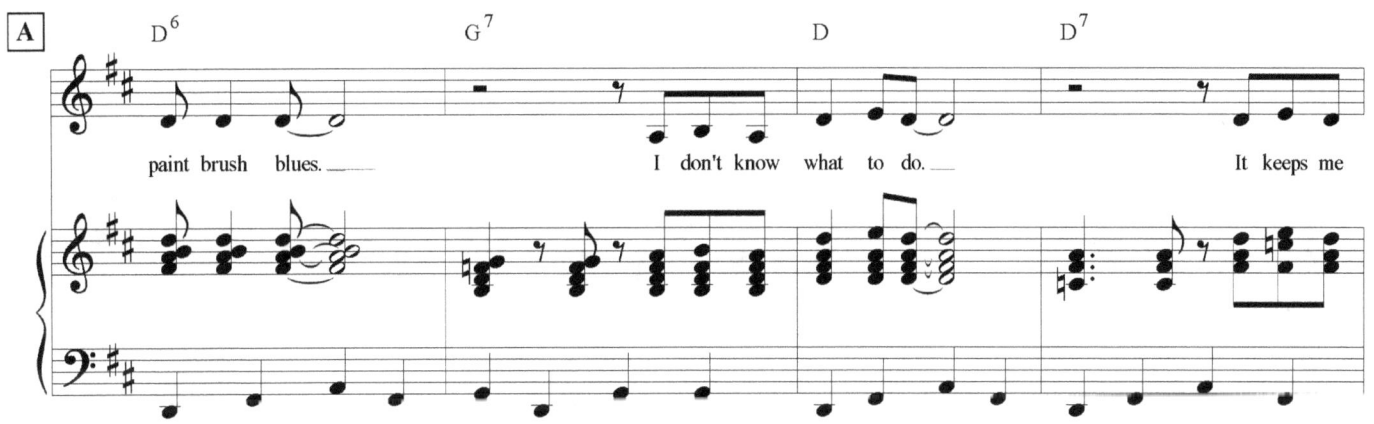

COPYRIGHT © 2016 L. Landolfi and Boumpani Music Co. ASCAP

Paint Brush Blues

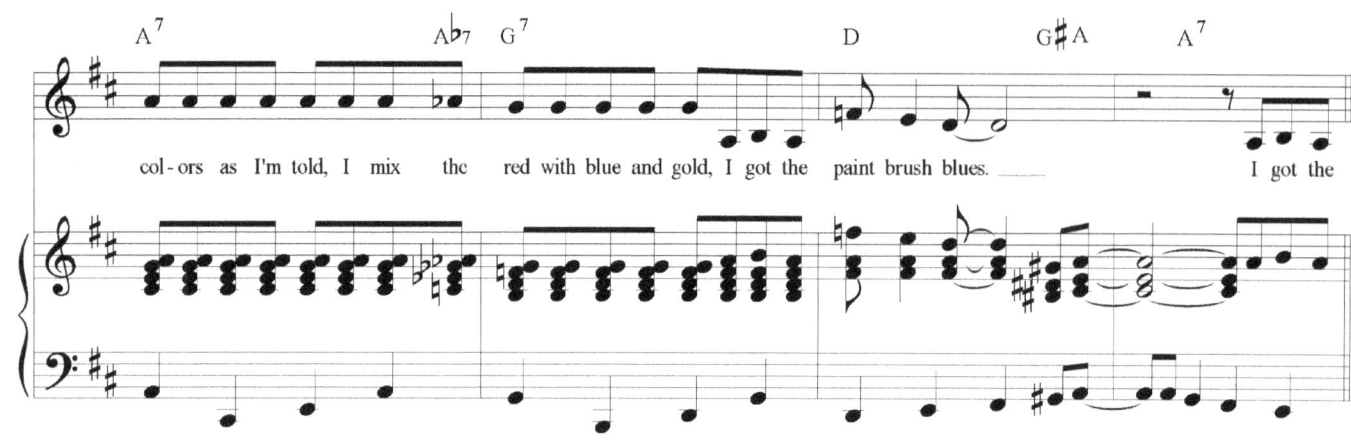

Paint Brush Blues

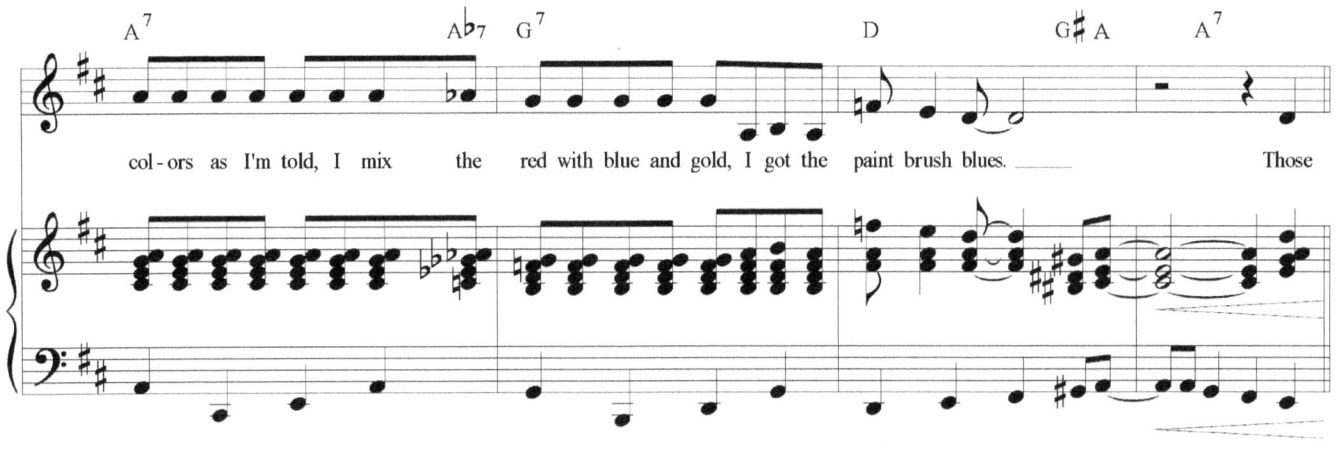

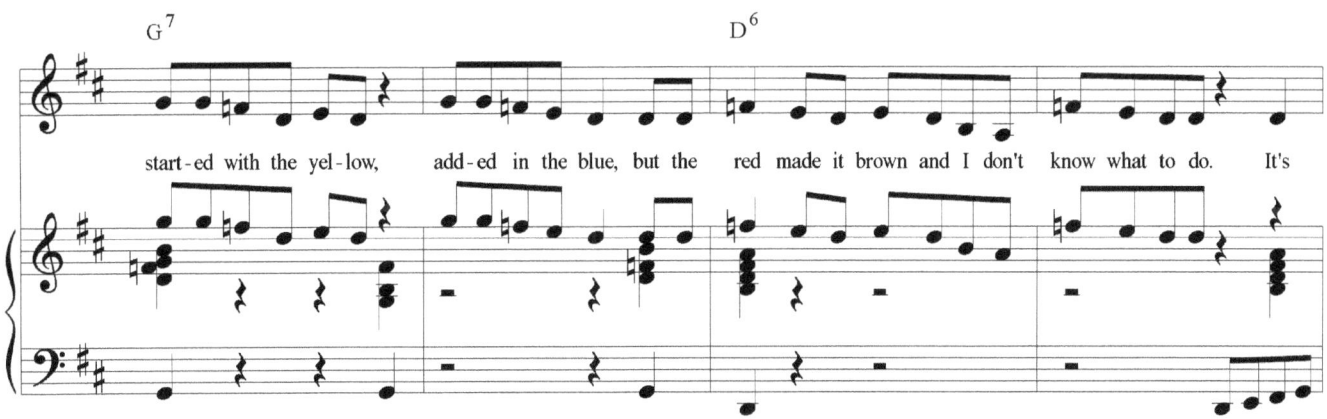

Paint Brush Blues

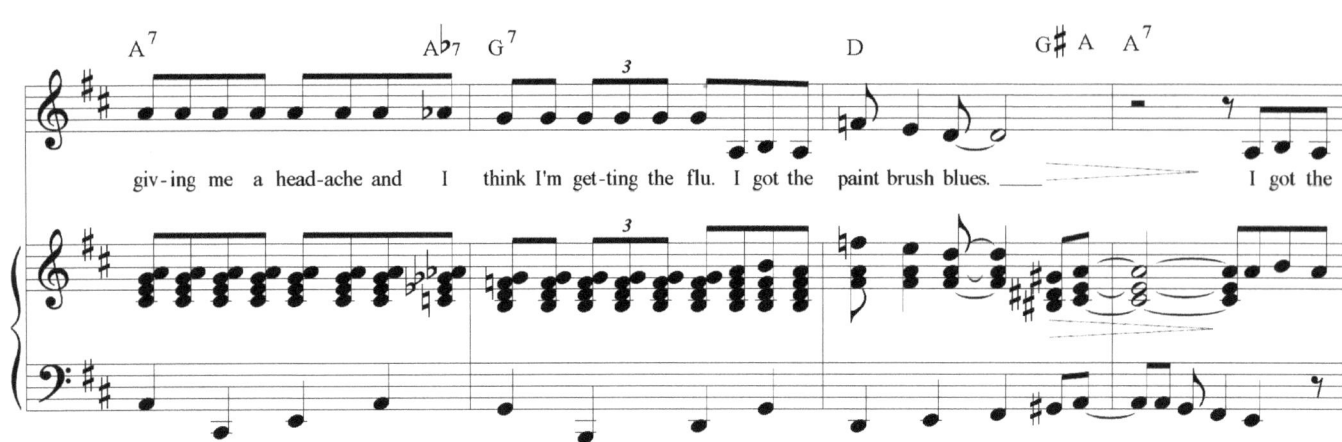

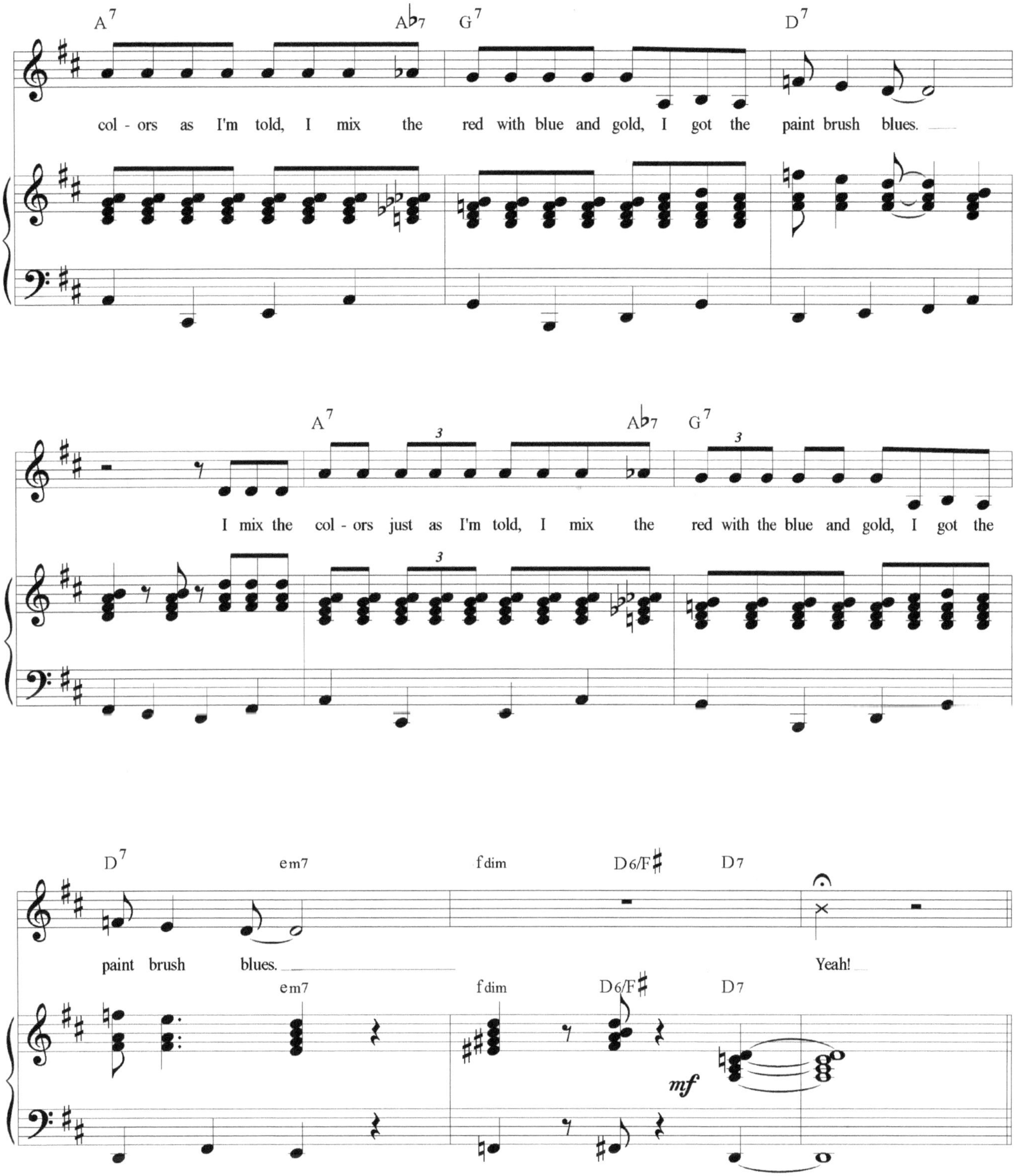
A7 Ab7 G7 D7
col - ors as I'm told, I mix the red with blue and gold, I got the paint brush blues.
A7 Ab7 G7
I mix the col - ors just as I'm told, I mix the red with the blue and gold, I got the
D7 em7 fdim D6/F# D7
paint brush blues.
Yeah!
em7 fdim D6/F# D7
mf

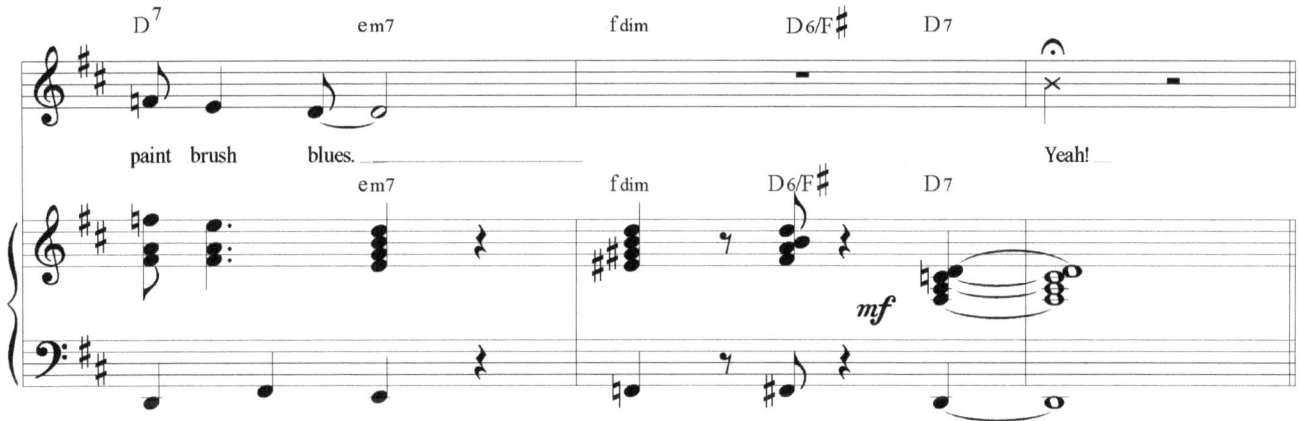

Personality

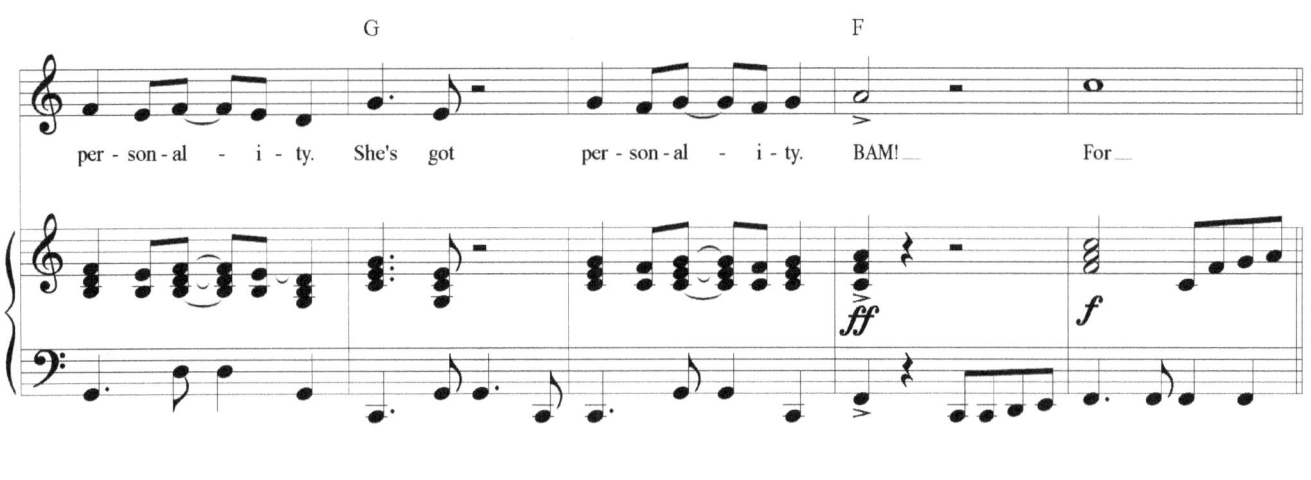

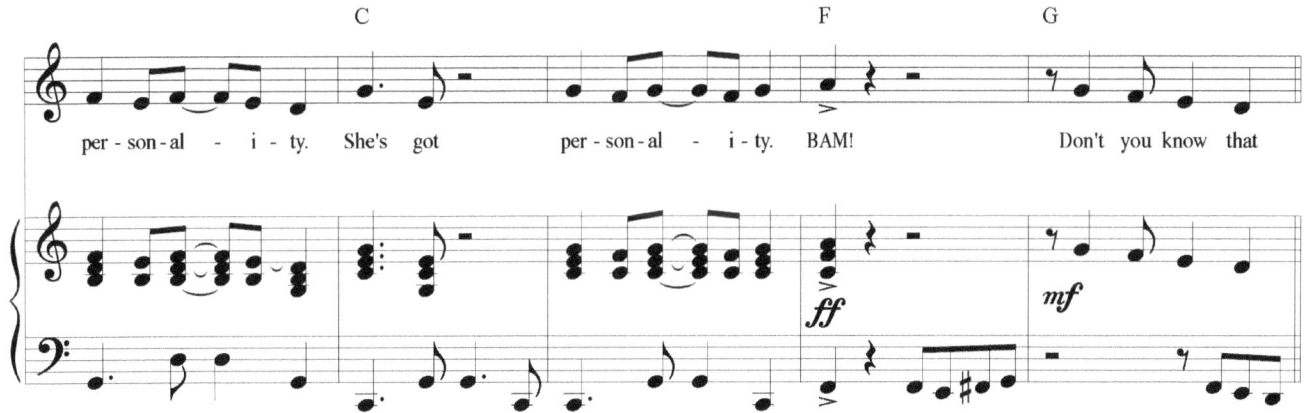

Personality

Personality

Personality

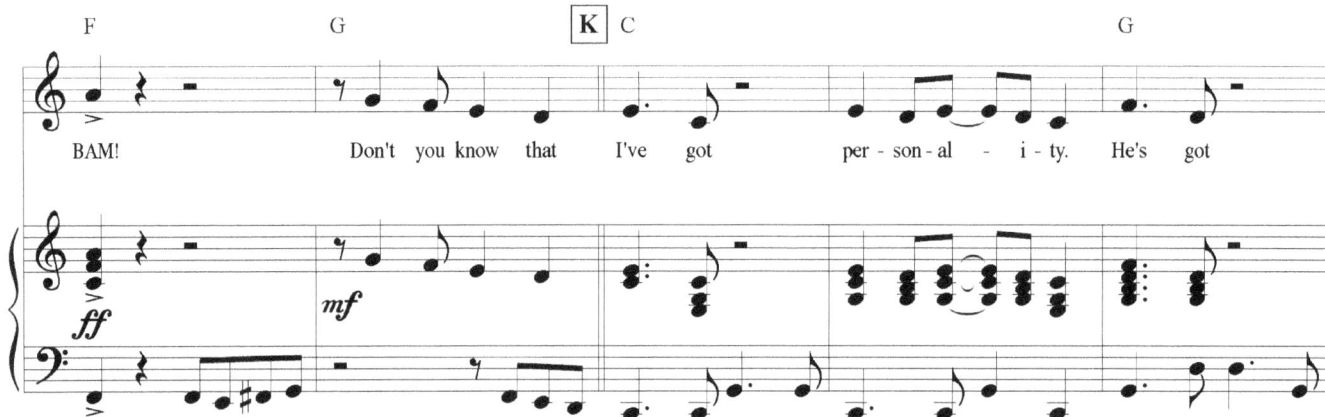

Personality

Please and Thank You

Words and Music by
Lea L. Landolfi

COPYRIGHT © 2016 L. Landolfi and Boumpani Music Co. ASCAP

Please and Thank You

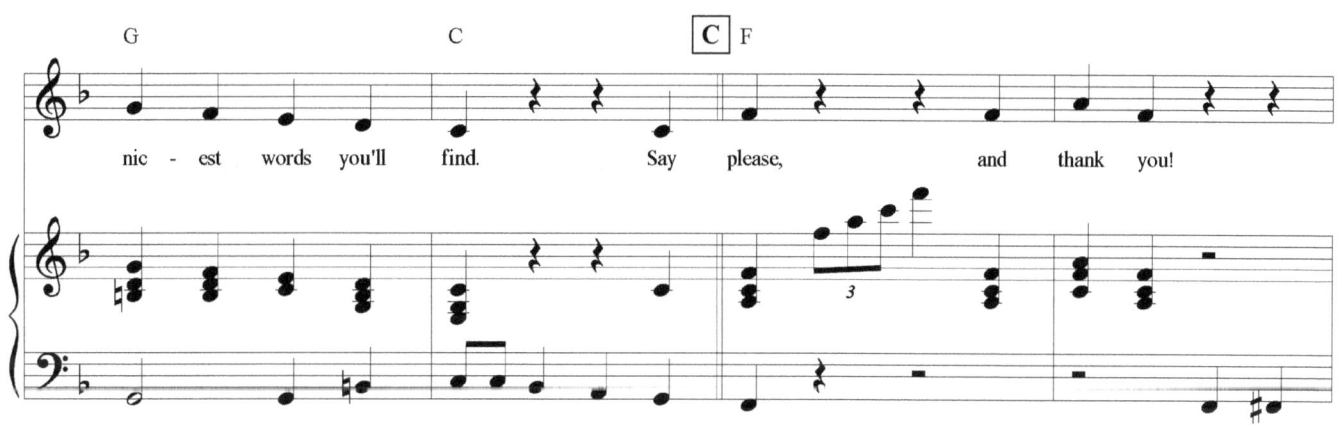

Please and Thank You

3

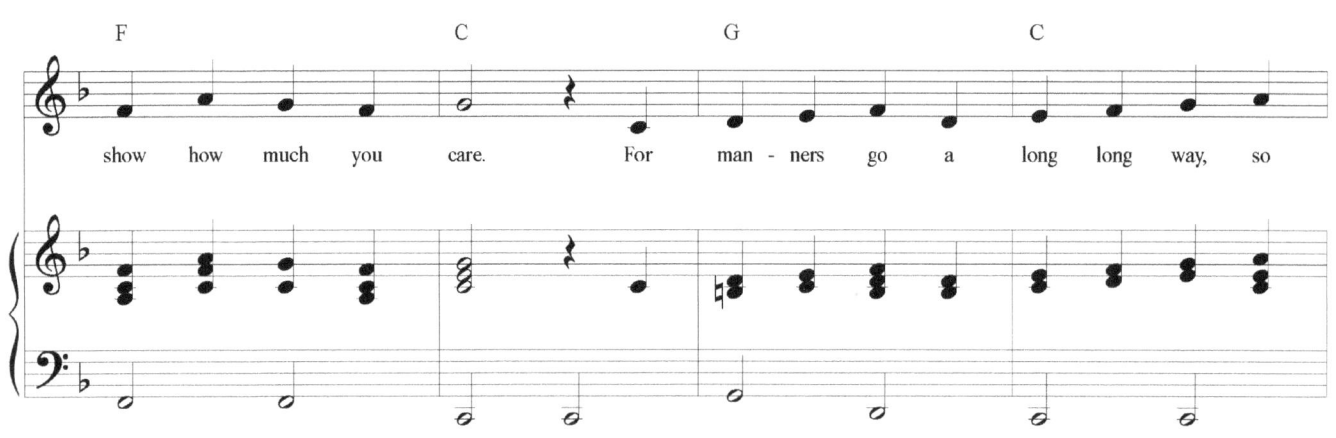
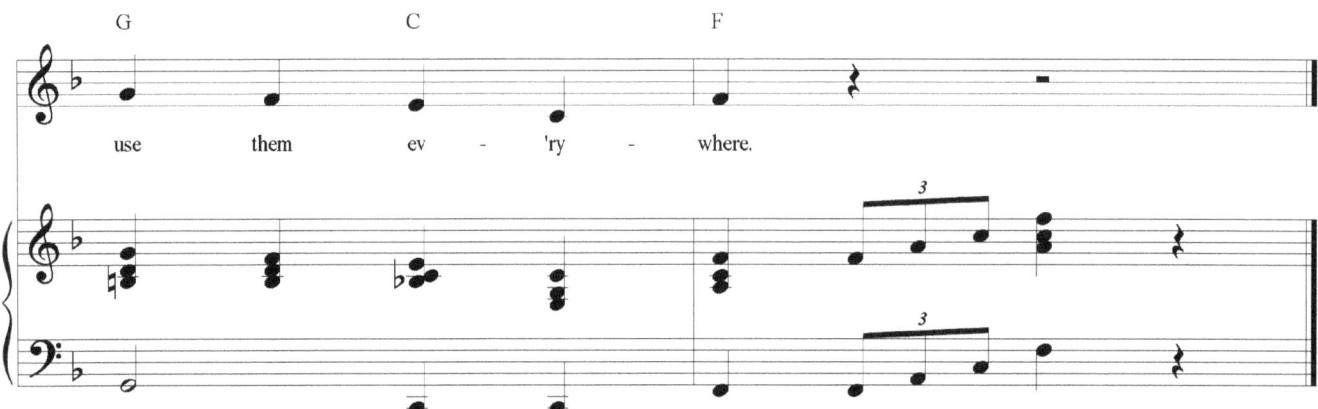

Rainbow

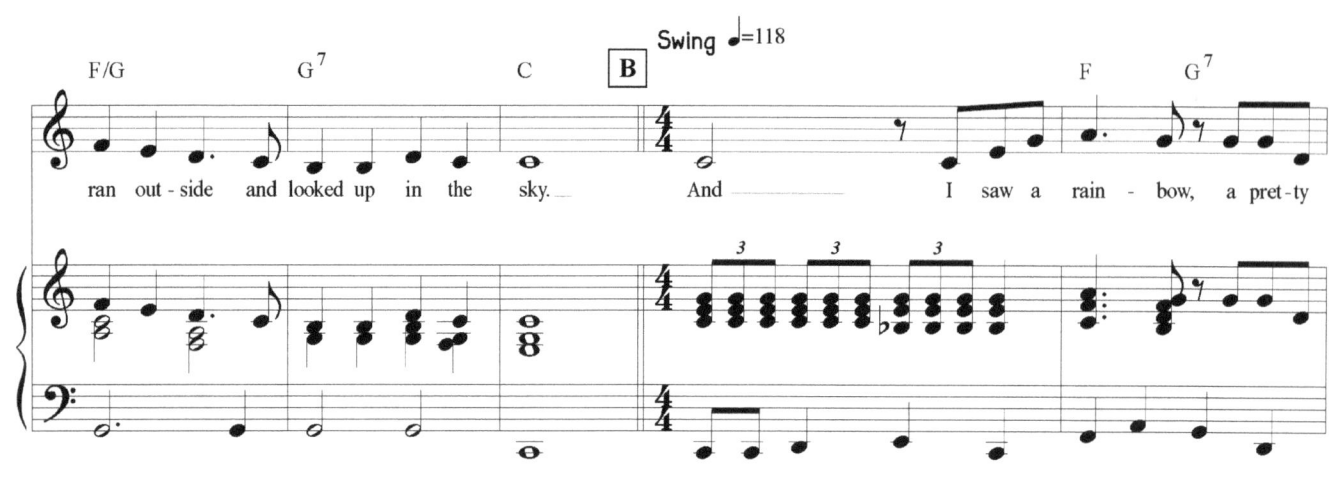

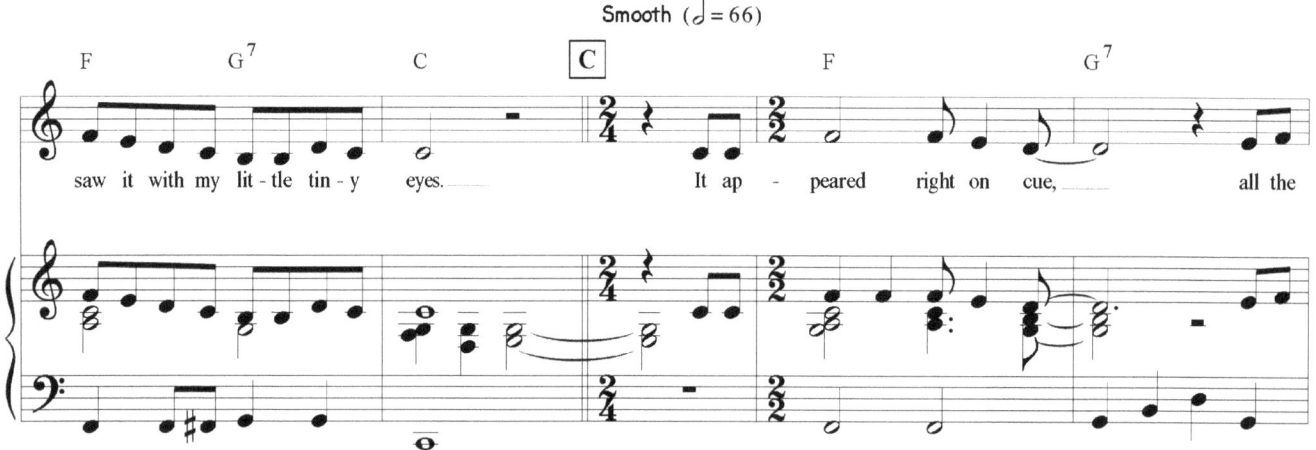

Rainbow

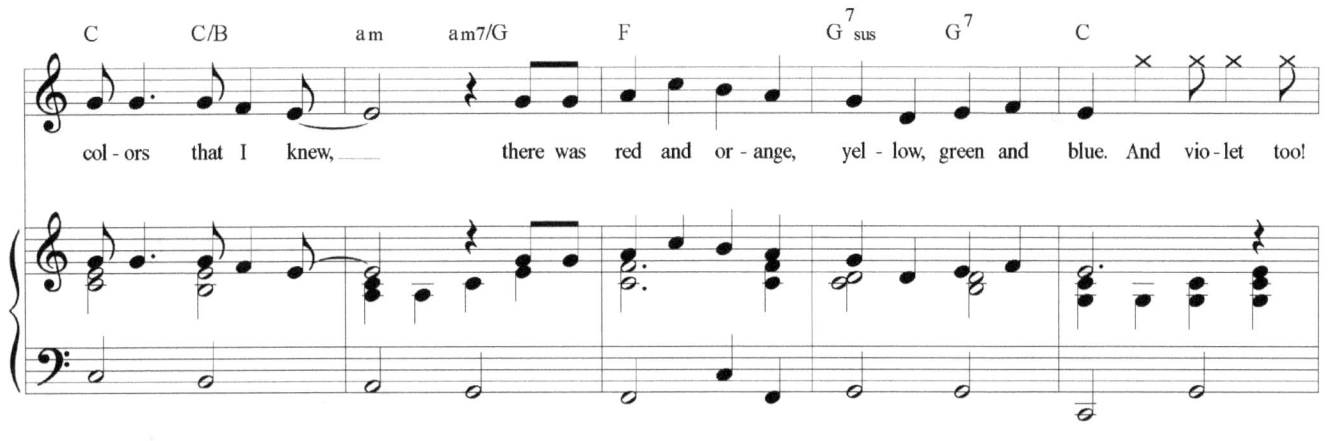

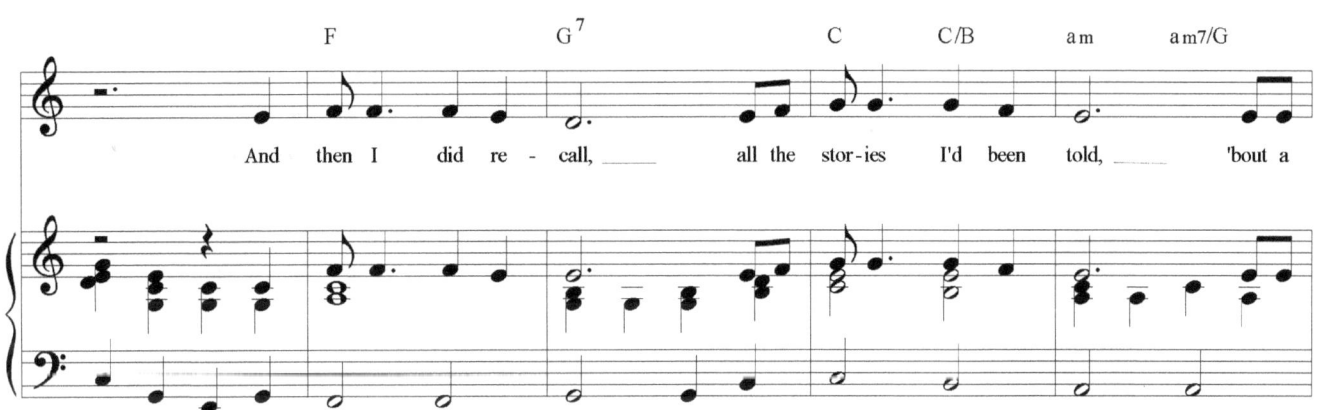

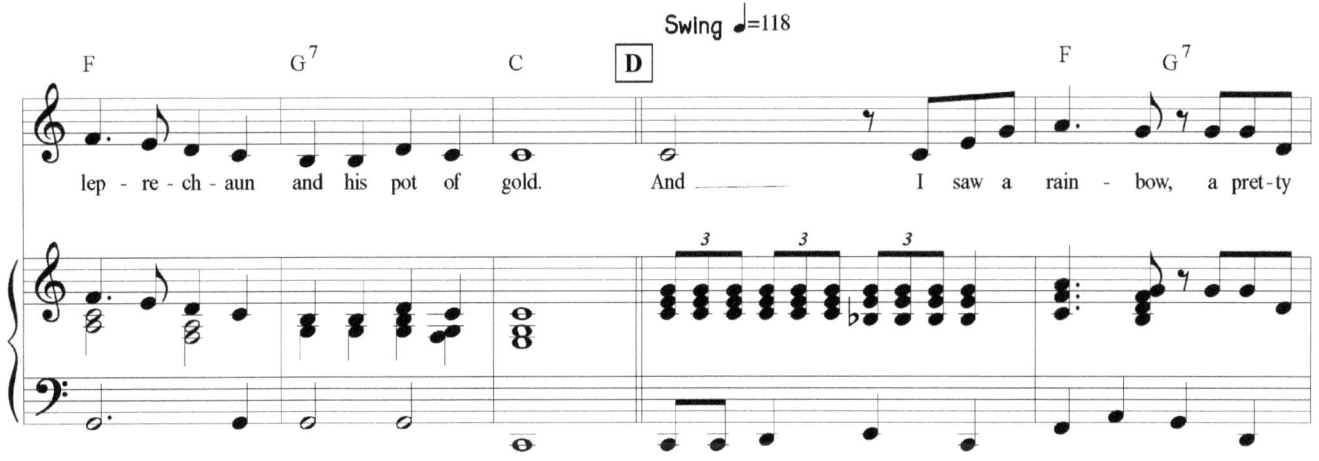

Rainbow

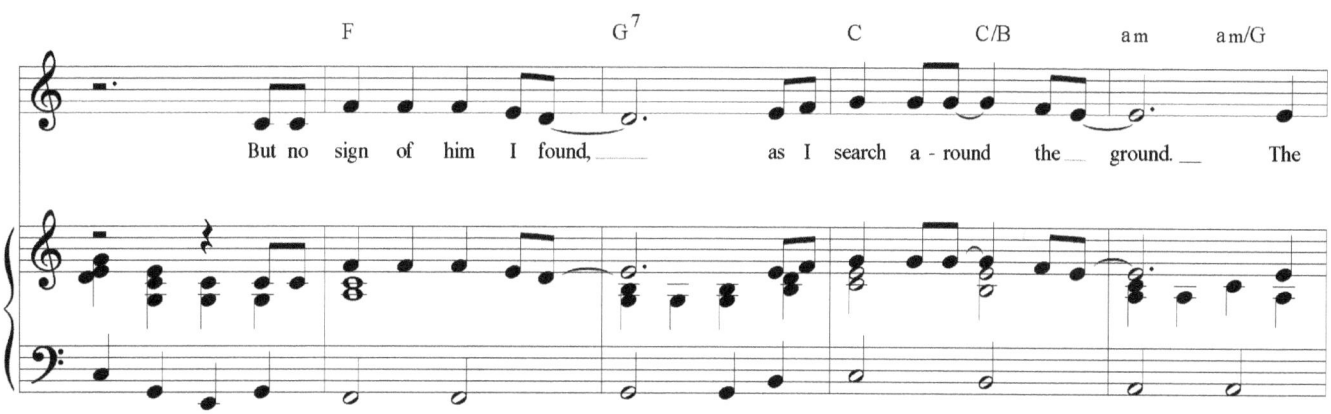

Rainbow

Rules, Rules, Rules!

Words and Music by Lea L. Landolfi

Rules, rules, so ma-ny rules! Why are there so ma-ny rules?

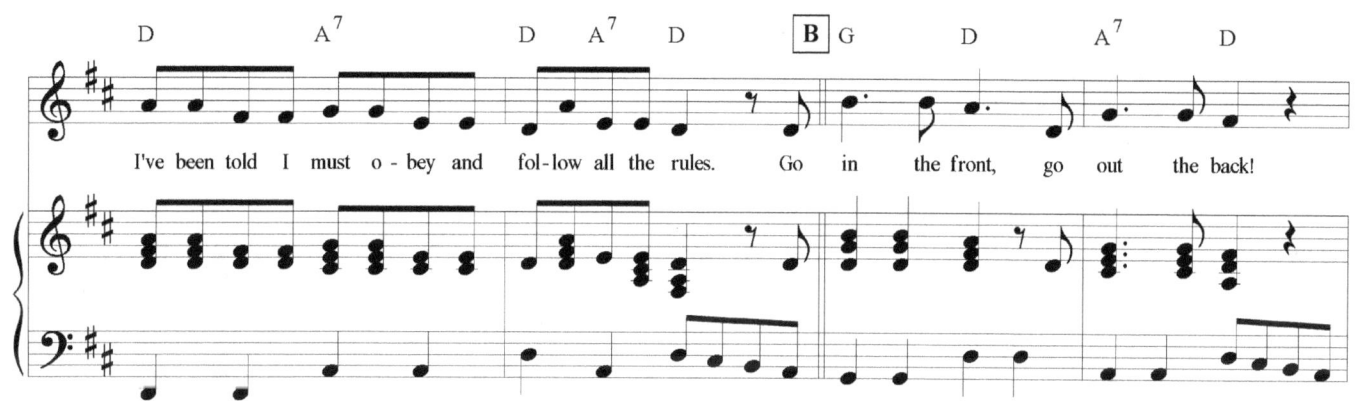

I've been told I must o-bey and fol-low all the rules. Go in the front, go out the back!

Walk this way, and not like that! Keep off the grass and do not run! Rules stop us from

COPYRIGHT © 2016 L. Landolfi and Boumpani Music Co. ASCAP

Rules, Rules

Rules, Rules

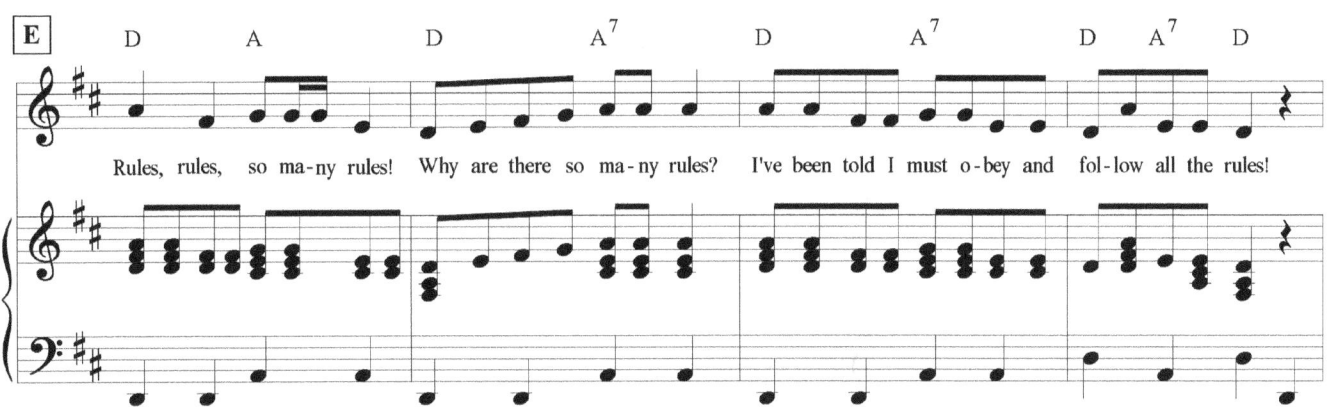
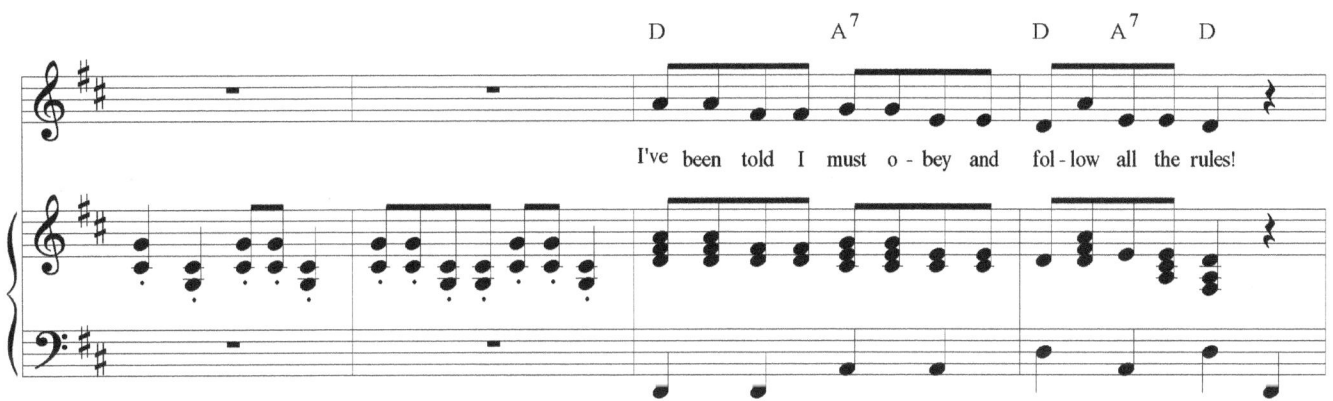

Smile

Words and Music by Lea L. Landolfi

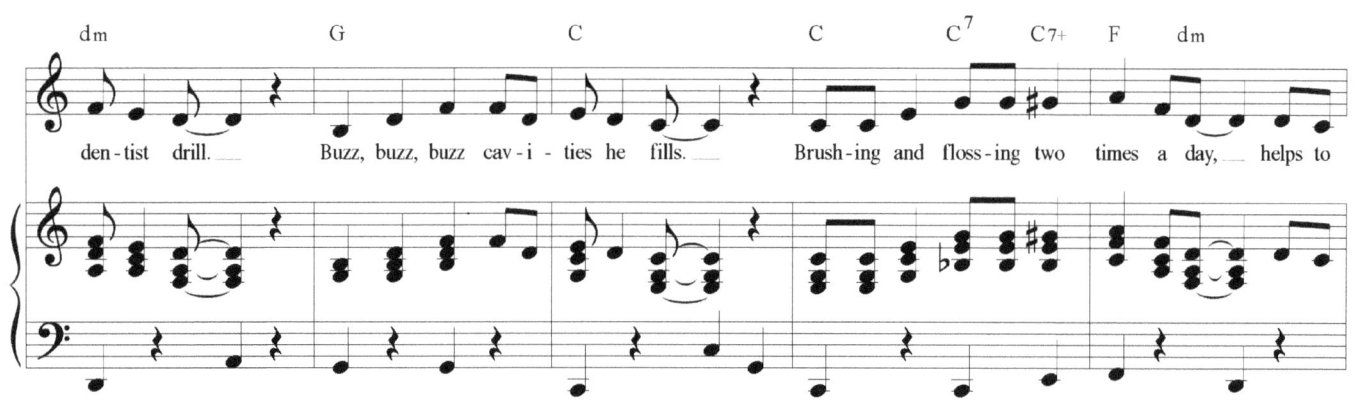
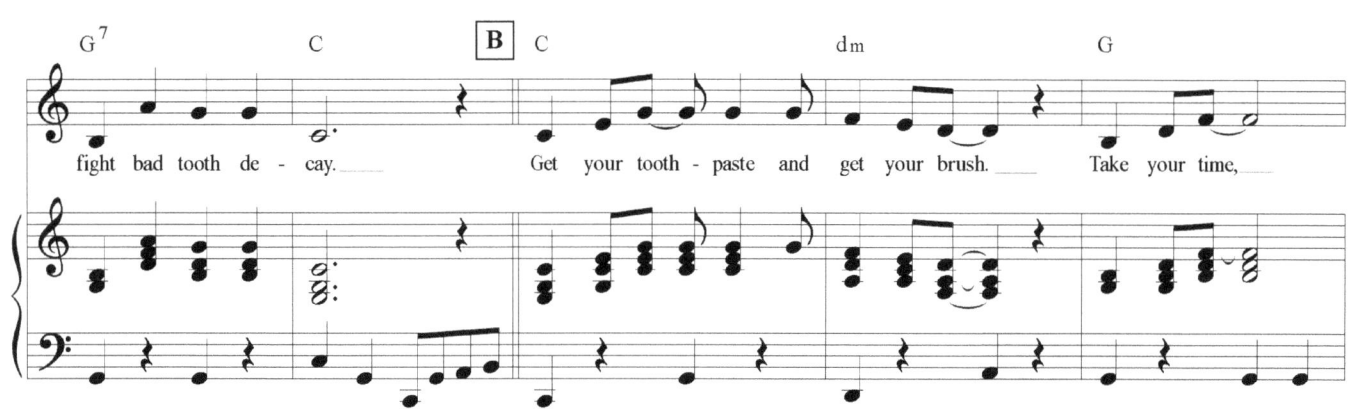

COPYRIGHT © 2016 L. Landolfi and Boumpani Music Co. ASCAP

2 Smile

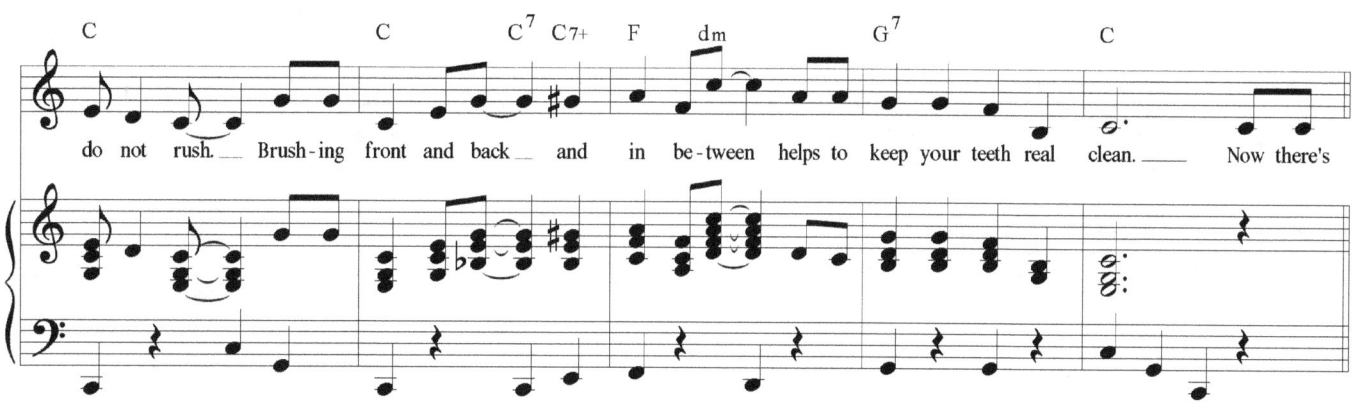
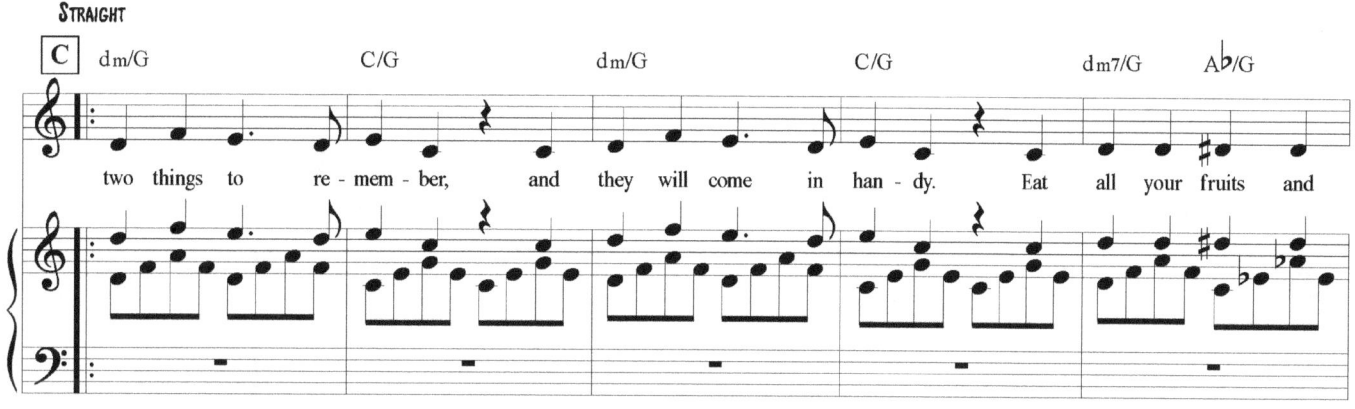
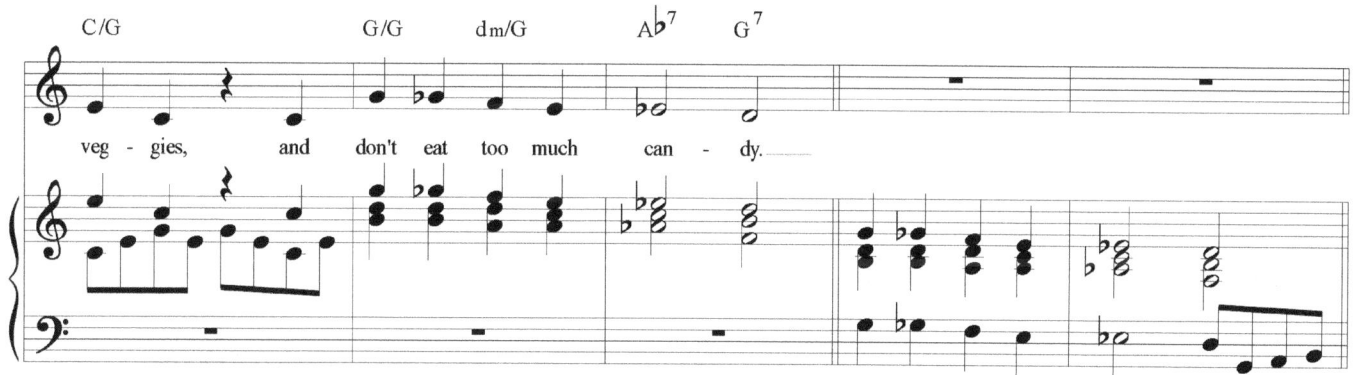

Smile

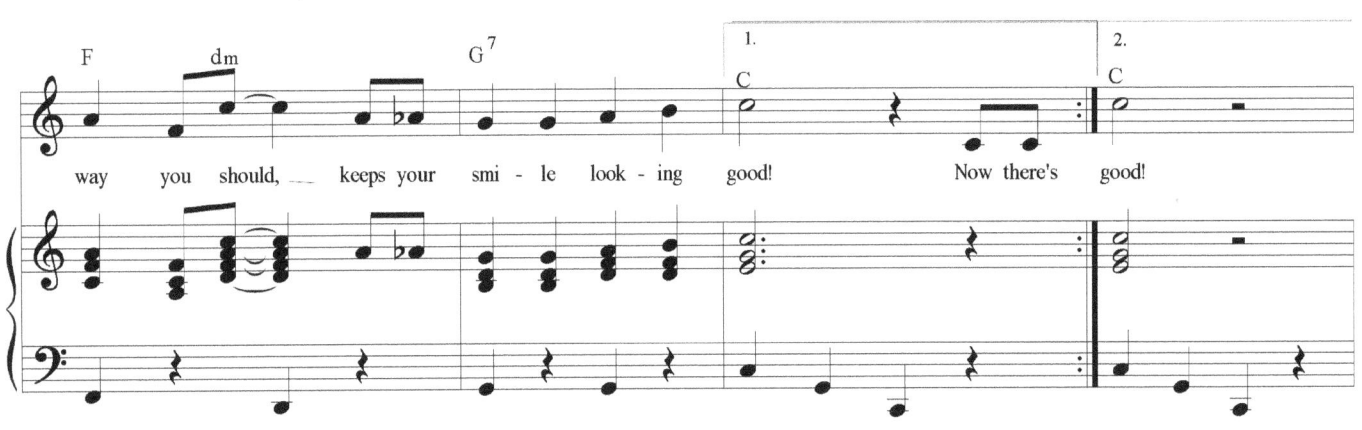

Steady Beat

Words and Music by Lea L. Landolfi

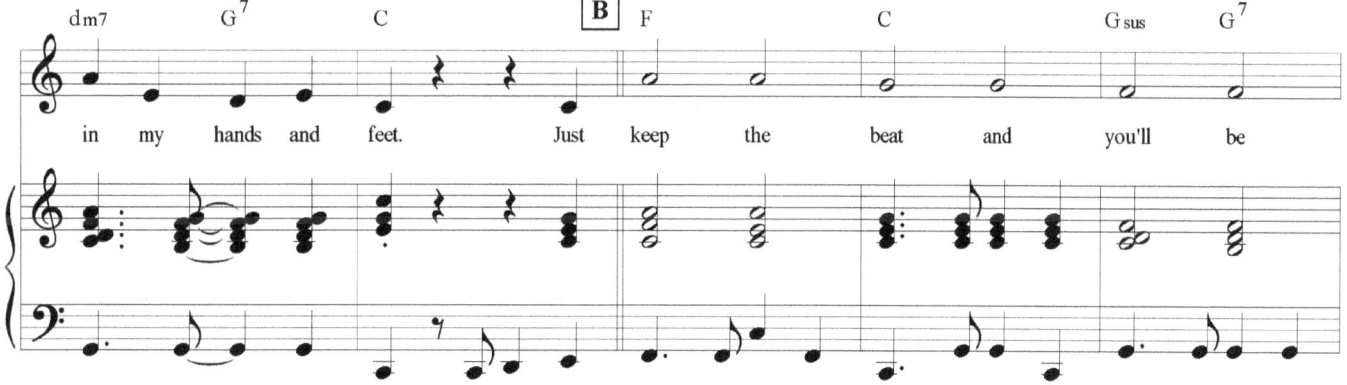

COPYRIGHT © 2016 L. Landolfi and Boumpani Music Co. ASCAP

Steady Beat

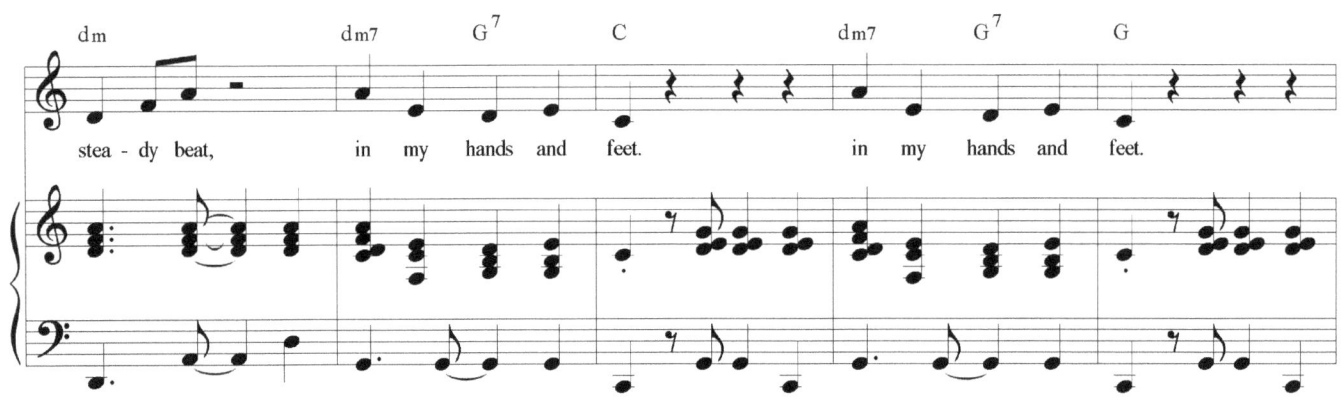

Steady Beat

Tell the Truth

Words and Music by
Lea L. Landolfi

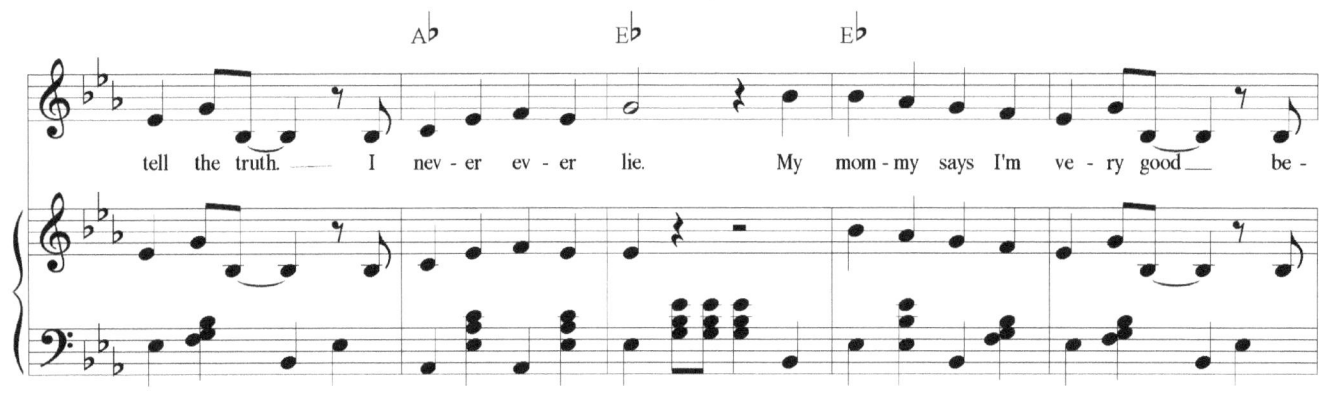
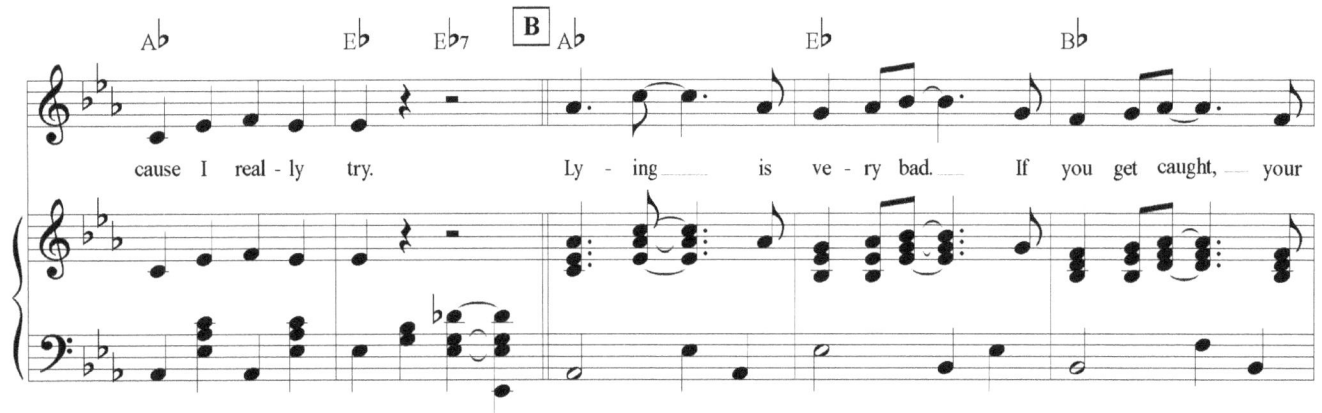

COPYRIGHT © 2016 L. Landolfi and Boumpani Music Co. ASCAP

Tell the Truth

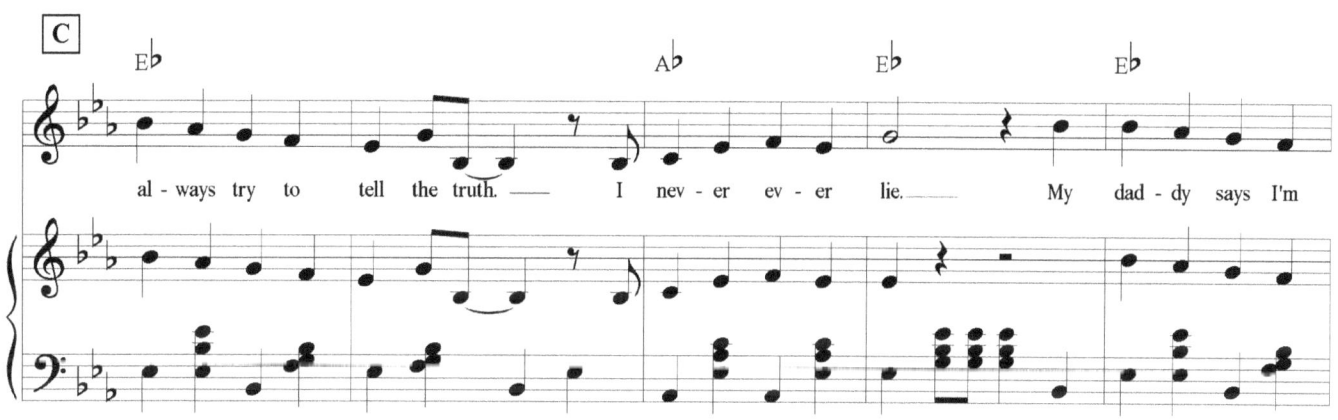

Tell the Truth

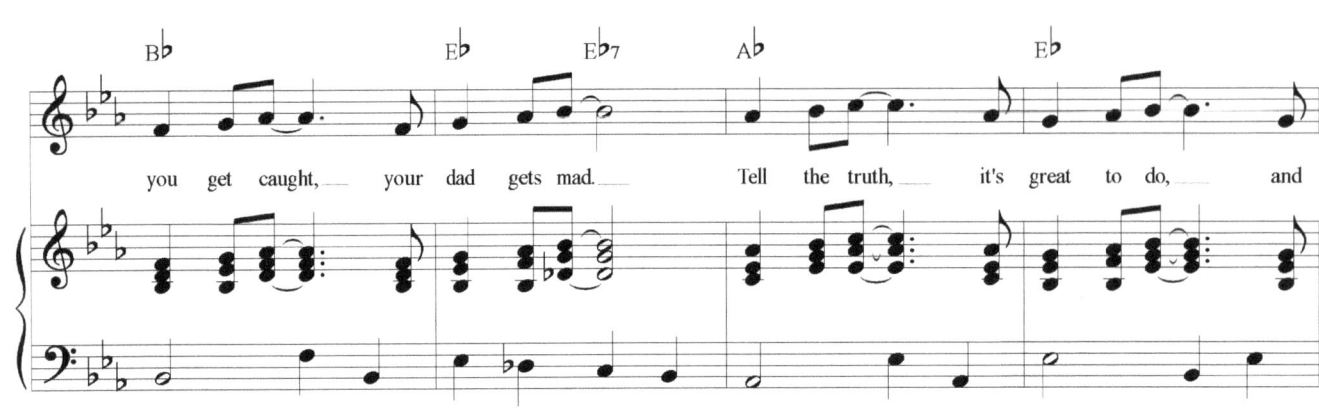
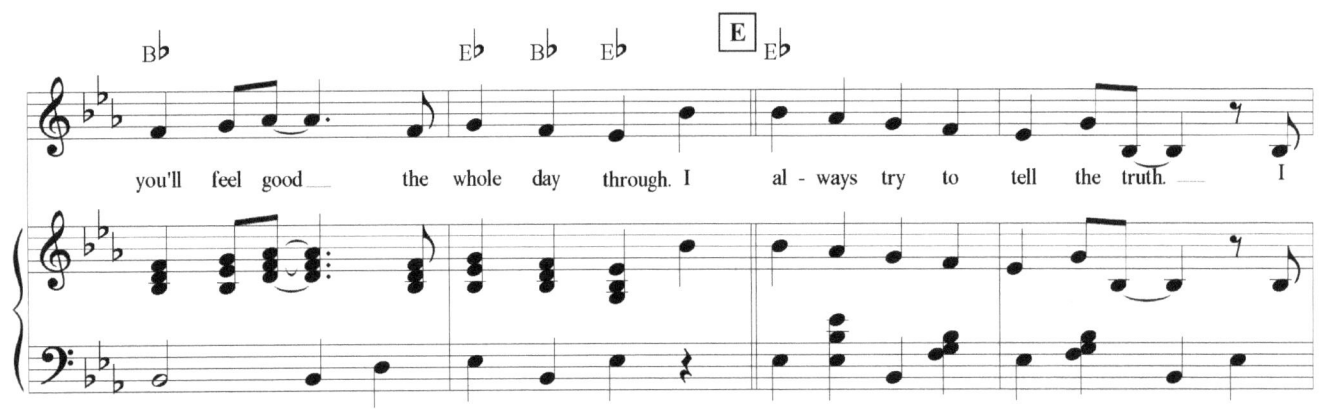

The Learning ChaCha

Words and Music by
Lea L. Landolfi

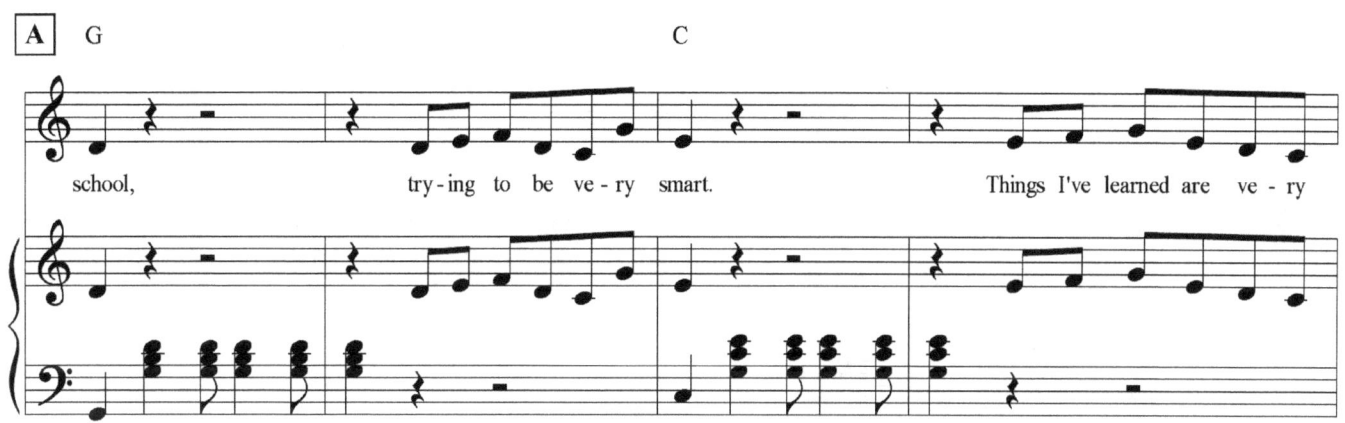

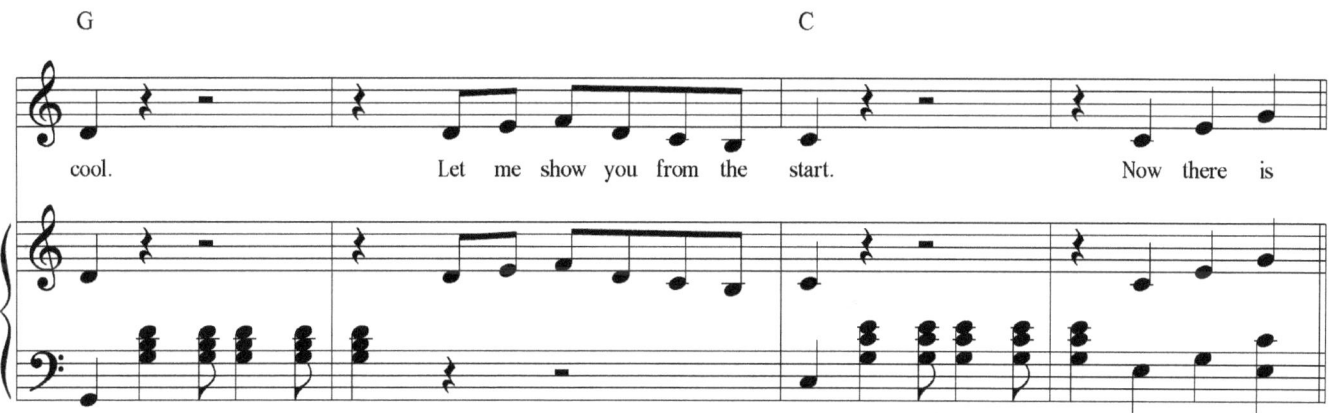

COPYRIGHT © 2016 L. Landolfi and Boumpani Music Co. ASCAP

The Learning ChaCha

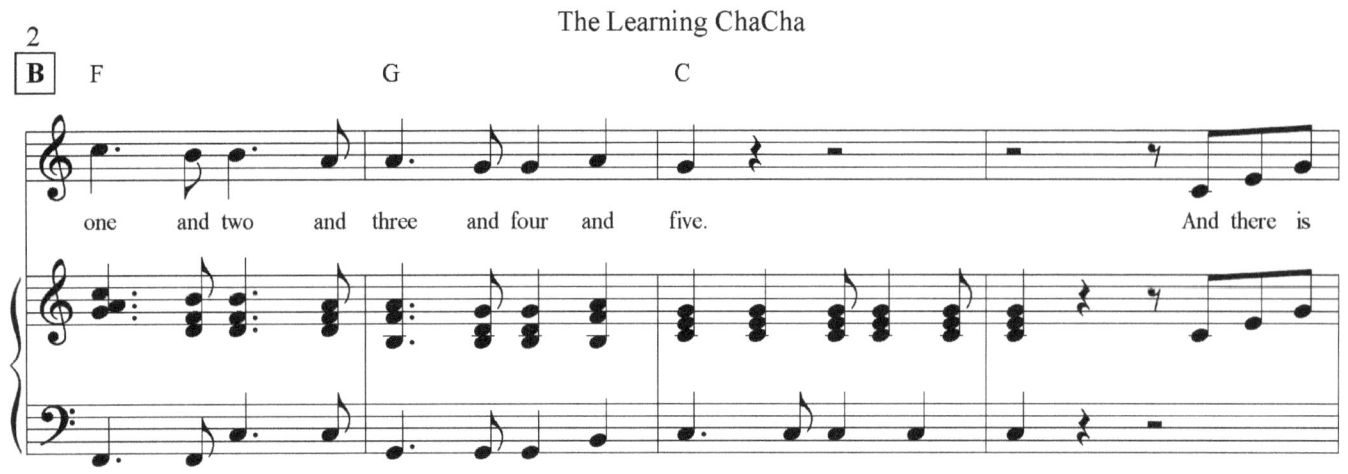

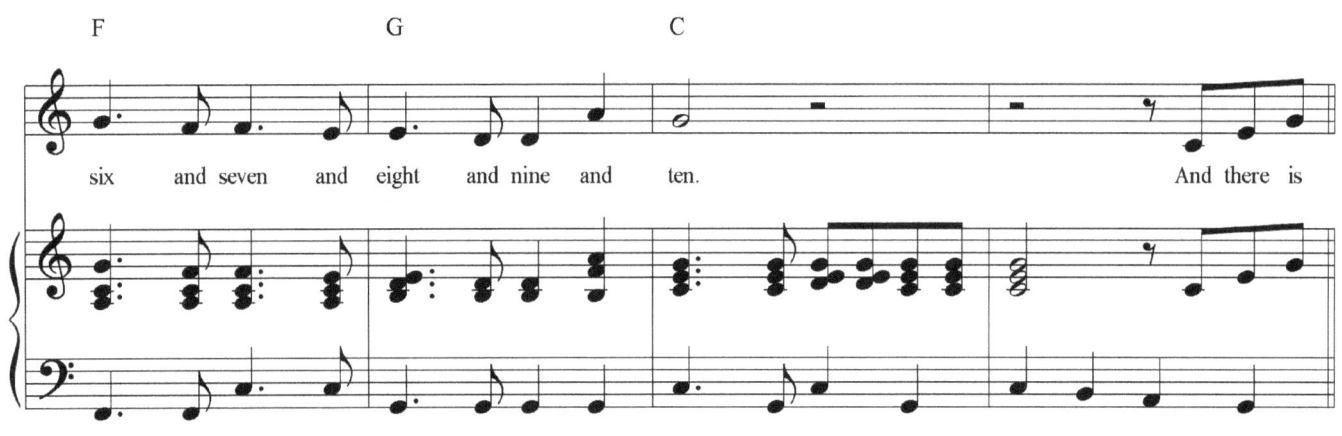

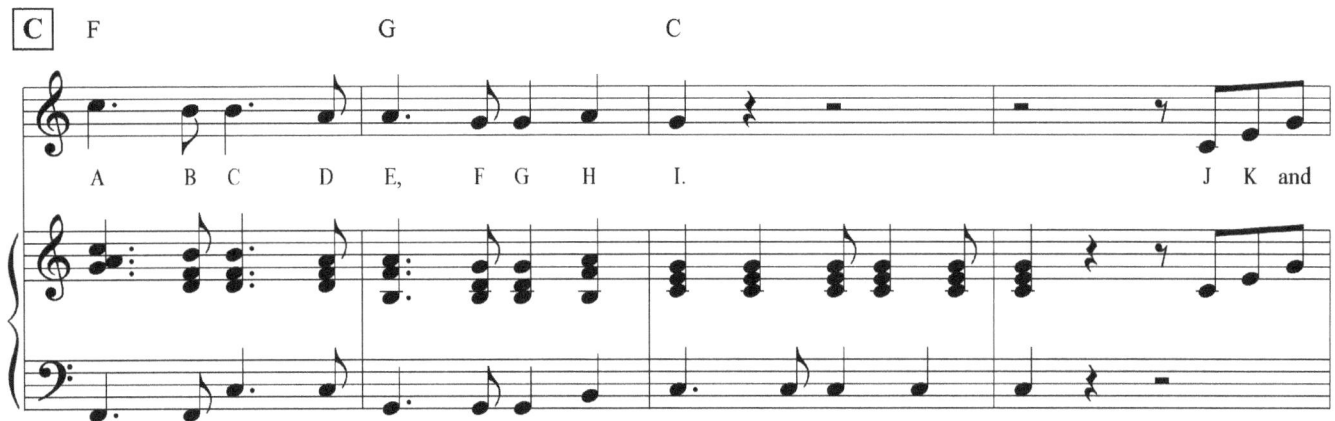

The Learning ChaCha

The Question

Words and Music by
Lea L. Landolfi

COPYRIGHT © 2016 L. Landolfi and Boumpani Music Co. ASCAP

The Question

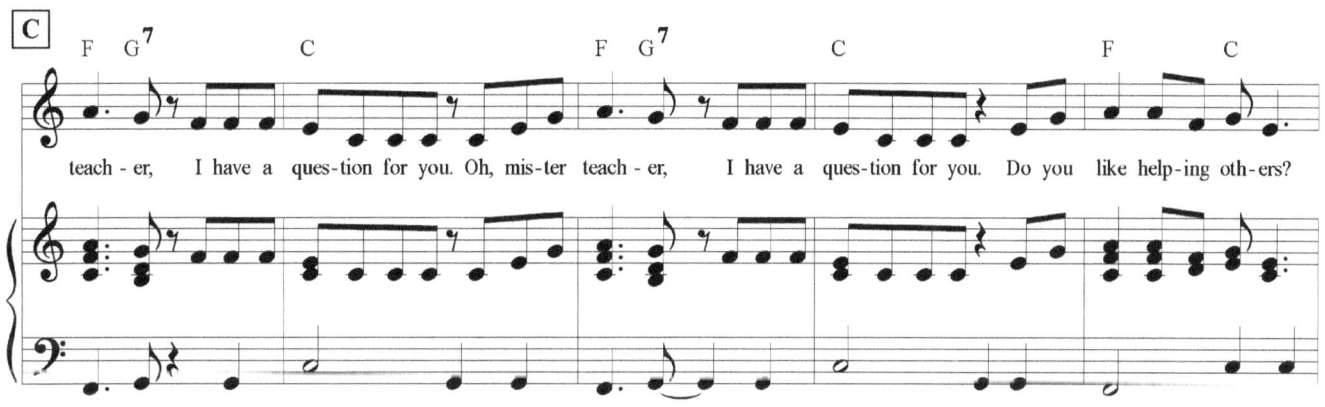

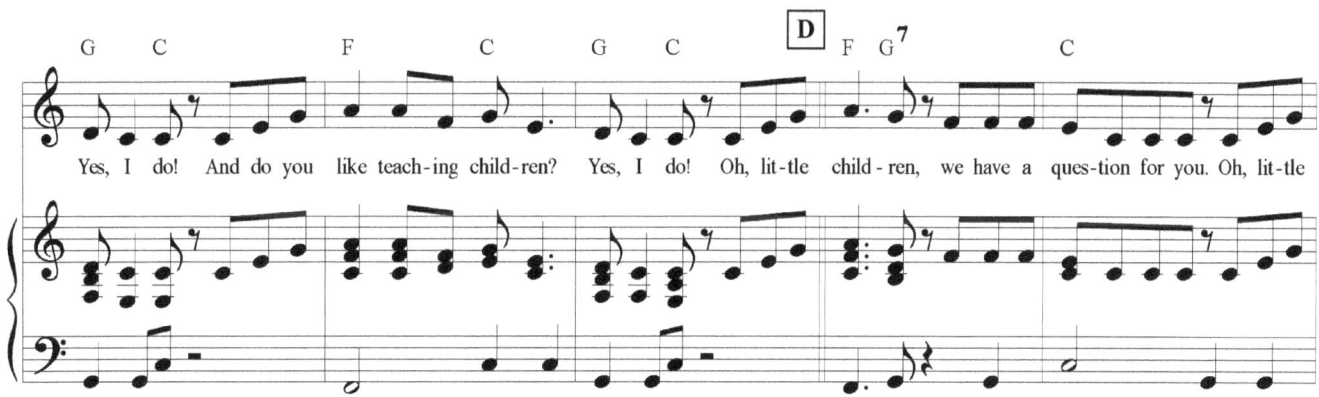

The Question

Train Ride

Words and Music by
Lea L. Landolfi

COPYRIGHT © 2016 L. Landolfi and Boumpani Music Co. ASCAP

When I Grow Up

Words and Music by Lea L. Landolfi

When I Grow Up

When I Grow Up

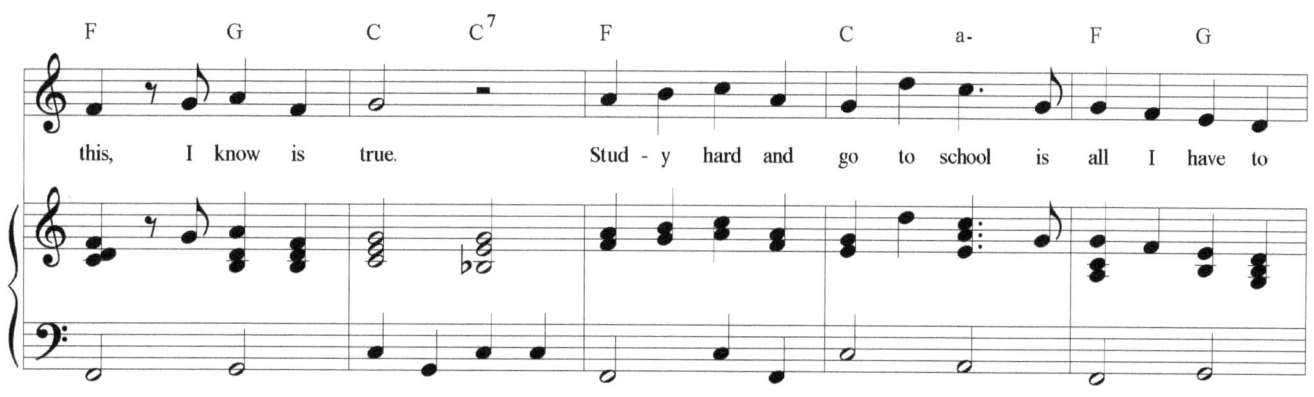

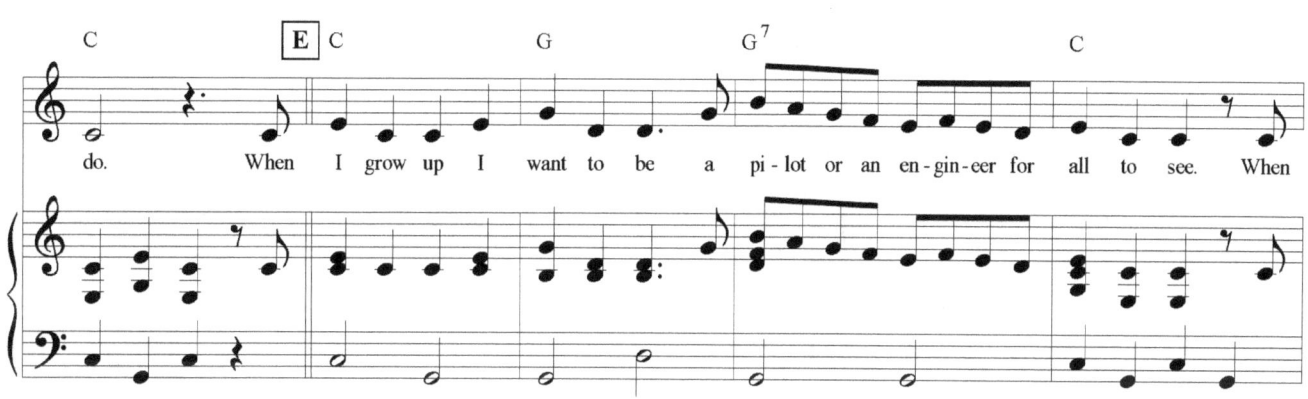

When I Grow Up

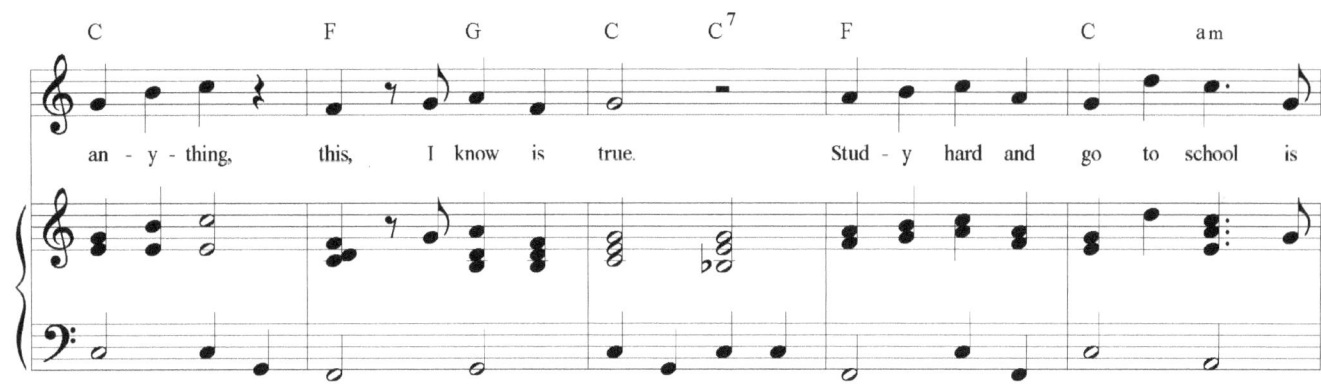

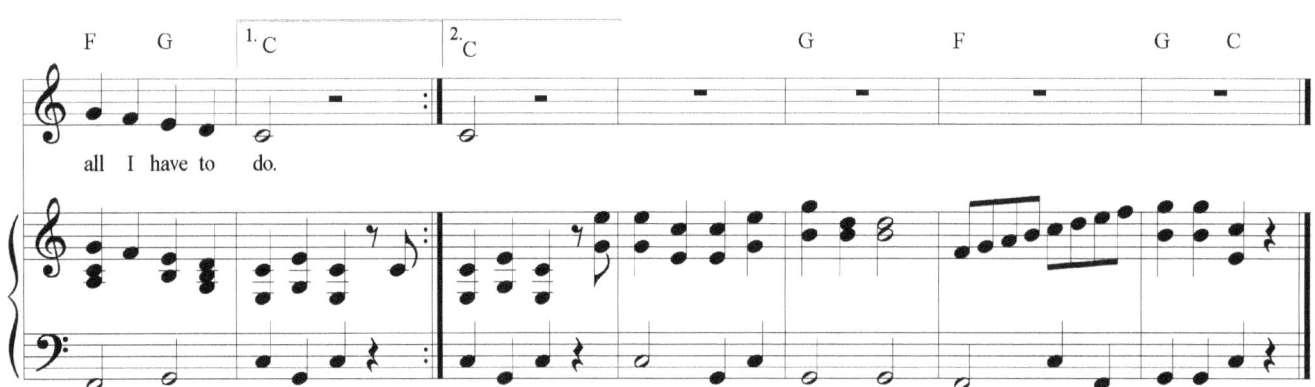

Suggested Grade Level Index

Songs Appropriate for Pre-K

Go To Bed, 18
Jump High, Jump Low, 22
Look Right, Look Left, 32
Number Fun, 40
Please and Thank You, 50
Steady Beat, 60
Tell The Truth, 62

Songs Appropriate for Kindergarten

A Time for Everything, 4
Be A Good Friend, 6
Dance-a-mania, 10
Go To Bed, 18
Jump High, Jump Low, 22
Look Right, Look Left, 30
Number Fun, 40
Please and Thank You, 50
Steady beat, 60
Tell The Truth, 62
The Learning Cha Cha, 64
The Question, 66
Train Ride, 68

Songs Appropriate for 1st Grade

A Time for Everything, 4
Be A Good Friend, 6
Dance-a-mania, 10
Go To Bed, 18
Jump High, Jump Low, 22
Look Right, Look Left, 30
Rules, Rules, Rules, 56
Please and Thank You, 50
Steady beat, 60
Tell the Truth, 62
The Learning Cha-Cha, 64
The Question, 66
Train Ride, 68

Songs Appropriate for 2nd Grade

Be A Good Friend, 6
Dance-a-mania, 10
Doin' My Best, 12
Eat Right, 16
How Are You?, 20
Let's Play, 26
My Family, 38
Personality, 46
Rules, Rules, Rules, 56
Smile, 58
The Question, 66
Train Ride, 68
When I Grow Up, 70

Songs Appropriate for 3rd Grade

A Reggae Day, 2
Be Nice Rap, 8
Doin' My Best, 12
Doodles, 14
Eat Right, 16
How Are You?, 20
Let's Play, 26
Move, Move, Move, 32
My Family, 36
Paint Brush Blues, 42
Personality, 46
Rainbow, 52
Smile, 58
When I Grow Up, 70

Songs Appropriate for 4th Grade

A Reggae Day, 2
Be Nice Rap, 8
Doodles, 14
Eat Right, 16
How Are You?, 20
Let's Play, 26
Move, Move, Move, 32
My Family, 36
Paint Brush Blues, 42
Personality, 46
Rainbow, 52
Smile, 58

Alphabetical Index

A
A Reggae Day, 2
A Time for Everything, 4

B
Be A Good Friend, 6
Be Nice Rap, 8

D
Dance-a-mania, 10 Doin'
My Best, 12 Doodles, 14

E
Eat Right, 16

G
Go to Bed, 18

H
How Are You?, 20

J
Jump High, Jump Low, 22

L
Let's Play, 26
Look Right, Look Left, 30

M
Move, Move, Move, 32
My Family, 36

N
Number Fun, 40

P
Paint Brush Blues, 42
Personality, 46
Please and Thank you, 50

R
Rainbow, 52
Rules, Rules, Rules, 56

S
Smile, 58
Steady beat, 60

T
Tell the Truth, 62
The Learning Cha-Cha, 64
The Question, 66
Train Ride, 68

W
When I Grow Up, 70

Notes

Notes

www.ingramcontent.com/pod-product-compliance
Lightning Source LLC
Chambersburg PA
CBHW080924170426
43201CB00016B/2253